The Money Making Confessions Of A Semi-Formal Tramp

By John Harrison

Published by
Streetwise Publications Ltd.

"*The Money Making Confessions*
Of A Semi-Formal Tramp"

Copyright © John D Harrison

The right of John D Harrison to be identified as the author of this work has been asserted by him in accordance with the Copyright, Designs and Patents Act 1998

First Published in Great Britain by

Streetwise Publications Ltd
Eden House
Sheffield Road
Rotherham
South Yorkshire
S60 1DX

Telephone: 01709 820033 Fax: 01709 360611
www.streetwisepublications.co.uk

A catalogue for this book is available from the British Library

ISBN 978-0-9557435-4-2

Printed in the UK by J F Print Ltd., Sparkford, Somerset

INDEX

INDEX

Introduction

So here I am, surrounded by reams of paper - the raw material from which the book you're about to read is constructed - wondering what it is that will bind it all together. And all I can come up with is glue.

You see, one of the great things about being 'your own boss' (in fact the *greatest* thing about being your own boss) is that nobody can tell you what to do. And that means you get to write about pretty much anything you want. There's no publisher to wag a disapproving finger, or implore you to stick to the plan when you drift off into the realms of personal vexation or vendetta. And so that's precisely what you do. But the downside of that situation becomes apparent when you sit down with what you've written, and wonder, "What the heck is all this about then?"

Most of what follows is taken from newsletters and articles I've written and prepared over the past few months, together with quite a bit of brand new material which has yet to see the light of day. The intention has always been to inform, empower and entertain – although not necessarily in that order. My underlying goal is unrelentingly consistent though – to guide you gently (and occasionally crudely) towards total financial independence.

Heck, I want to make you rich!

I realise this may not be immediately apparent when you find yourself in the midst of a long winded rant about Canarian Bananas, Kosovans at car boot sales or idiots in Ikea. It may appear a distant speck on a far off horizon as you find yourself diverted to a toilet in Lincoln in the company of a giant with digestive transit issues. But stick with it. These are distractions you must endure on the road to enlightenment. There are important messages in there somewhere. I promise.

They're messages I've been pressing home for almost 20 years now – and with a fair degree of success. It's always nice when someone gets in touch to say that they've enjoyed what you've written, but even better when they write to say that it's transformed their lives. And it's fair to say that when someone has made a few million pounds, their life has been transformed. That seems to happen quite a lot.

I've dedicated the first few chapters to helping you get the foundations right. You see if your underlying attitudes influences and beliefs are wrong, it doesn't really matter what business or enterprise you embark upon – it doesn't matter what neat marketing strategies or tricks you learn about. Nothing is going to work out for you, because like a house built on sand, your enterprise will quickly sink without trace.

And while I'm in pious preaching mode, another word of warning - No matter what you glean or learn within the pages of this book – or indeed any other – it's both useless and impotent without action. You won't change your life by reading. That only comes about by taking enthusiastic action with what you've read. And going back a stage from there that only happens when you approach what you read with an open mind and a belief that it can be done.

Fortunately, I have a major advantage which helps instil this belief in anybody. After reading my material, the most common reaction is "Well if *he* can do it, ANYBODY can!" If I do no more than convince you that even someone almost universally incompetent can become wealthy – then the time invested writing this book will have been well spent.

You don't need to be 'special' to get rich, but you do need to be different – or to be more precise, you need to do things differently. Do what everyone else does and guess what? You gct what everyone else gets. If you're happy with that, you can stop reading now – but I suspect you want more. Most of us do. I know that what follows can be an important stepping stone in helping you get it.

So let's get started...

Norm In The USA

I first visited the United States in 1984. I'd just been made redundant two days before Christmas, (no please, put the violins away, it wasn't that bad) but managed to get another job with the UK subsidiary of an American company straight away. In an attempt to convince me that there was more to the company than the rented three room office above an estate agents they currently occupied, I was sent to the company HQ in Massachusetts and then on to New York. I loved it.

I've been back to the States quite a few times since, and with the exception of the one time when I inexplicably and uncharacteristically got married in Las Vegas, it's always been an enjoyable and enriching experience. Things do get a little strange from time to time though, not least because the common language always leads me into a false sense of security. I expect them to be like us, but they're not.

A few weeks ago we went over for a family holiday in Florida, and stayed in a hotel linked to the Orange County Convention Centre in Orlando. Now this place (like pretty much everything else in America) is huge. It makes the NEC in Birmingham look like a village hall. The hotel was packed with delegates for a convention taking place that week, which just happened to be...

Hurricane Preparedness and Debris Management 2010

I love the way Americans call a spade a....mobile earth relocation facilitator. Debris Management... marvellous! It was easy to imagine the distant conversations in the lobby. "So what line are you in?" "I'm in debris management – roofing material and body parts division...and you?" "Hurricane Preparedness...man and boy. Are you ready?"

I couldn't help wondering whether hurricane preparedness and debris management were one discipline or two separate ones brought together for this convention in a marriage of convenience. I suspect it's the latter, and then started to worry about what these debris management people do when there's no hurricane debris to manage. I imagined them sat huddled around their TV screens in an evening, monitoring the weather reports and rubbing their hands in glee at the first sign of a breath of wind.

Maybe they fill the time between hurricanes clearing up after rock festivals, or outside crappy kebab vans on a Saturday night. From what I've seen, the level of devastation is very similar. Or maybe they just fill their time cruising from one debris management conference to another – meeting up with identikit Debris Management specialists who are all called Gus…all have a Walrus moustache, all wear yellow braces and all come from Wisconsin. Wherever that is.

Now the thing about all these conference delegates (and indeed large swathes of the US population in general) is that like their buildings – they are huge. I'm not talking about a bit of a spare tyre here. I'm talking the sort of huge that had forced the hotel I was staying in (presumably following an embarrassing incident involving a crowbar, some KY jelly and a winch) to make the chairs in the restaurant easily wide enough for two average arses. There were very few average arses to be seen though. And it's not hard to see why.

Order a portion of anything in the States and it will be at least twice as big as the same thing in the UK. Why have a plate of chicken for goodness sake, when you can have a bucket? Why have a bag of crisps, when you can have a small sack instead? Why have one pancake when you can have 12 at the 'all you can eat for $5 buffet? These are questions that many Americans have clearly been asking themselves for years, and are struggling to find an answer.

The end result is that you'll see more 25 stone plus people in a single morning in America than you'll see in a year in the UK. And here's what interesting…after a very short time, it all seems so worryingly normal. In fact you start to feel a little under-nourished. Would it really be so bad to start eating more and put on a little weight? It can't be that bad can it? You're the odd one out, after all.

There's no big secret to what's going on here. In general, people want to 'fit in', and in order to do that they compare themselves with others around them. If you think about it, that's the only way to establish what's 'normal'. Spend a few days in a Florida convention hotel and your perception of what's a normal body weight takes a serious battering. Expose yourself to that sort of 'normality' for any longer, and you'd need to give some serious thought to how you'd regain your sense of perspective.

All very interesting, but what else is considered to be 'normal' in America?

Well for decades, the United States has been the economic power house of the world, and there's no doubt that this power house has been fuelled primarily by individual enterprise and endeavour. The entrepreneurial mindset is one that's considered normal in the United States. It's the American dream. People are ambitious. They're keen to progress financially. They want to get rich, and they're prepared to put in the effort to achieve it. Why is this?

I have a theory. I have no evidence to back it up, but if you think for one second that that will stop me inflicting it upon you, then you're sadly mistaken.

The United States is a relatively new country. With some notable exceptions, the people there (or at least their ancestors) arrived as individuals, and by choice. They could have stayed in the country of their birth, but chose to make the long journey west for what they hoped would be a better life. This in itself set them apart from the majority of the world's population. They got off their backsides and did something through individual action. This entrepreneurial spirit not only turned the US into a world power, but it was later passed down through multiple generations, and was adopted by other groups who did not originally arrive by choice, but who came to accept this entrepreneurial attitude as normal.

Now compare that with the UK. It's a much older country for a start. Most of our ancestors didn't arrive here as individuals seeking out a better life; they arrived as part of large invading groups. As such, they were primarily followers, tagging on to a few enterprising individuals and hoping to pick up a few scraps along the way. They were told what to do and they did it. Over the centuries, this tendency to follow was built upon through a class system which instilled in successive generations an ethos of knowing your place. Individual enterprise wasn't something for the likes of ordinary folk.

Many of those who arrived in the UK much later (in the second half of the 20th century) were not entrepreneurial in outlook either. They were low level manual workers brought in en masse to do jobs which the established population didn't want to do.

Of course this is a massive generalisation, and there are many exceptions. But what we're dealing with here is the general trends which have shaped the prevailing culture in the country with regard to entrepreneurship, wealth and endeavour. It's what makes the people who are around you, the way they are. And in the main, they are neither enterprising nor entrepreneurial.

The bottom line is that it's not 'normal' in the UK, to be strongly driven towards a desire to get rich through enterprise. It's not cool to be seen to be trying too hard either. And most of us are surrounded by folk (apparently well meaning family and friends) who will pour cold water on any ambitions we dare to mouth in that direction. It's just not normal. It's not for the likes of us.

Faced with being forced to go against the norm…and against our family and friends…is it any wonder that most of us give up before we've even started? We metaphorically resign ourselves to the bargain bucket, the all you can eat buffet and the double arse chair. We fall in with the crowd.

So what's to be done?

Well in the States, the entrepreneurial attitude prevails because it's the norm and its human nature to gravitate towards the norm. To emulate that, that we need to surround ourselves with people who we wish to copy, or who share our ambition. We need to associate with people for whom enterprise, endeavour and achievement are the norm. When we do that it becomes our norm too.

It sounds simple, but it can mean making some very hard choices. Your family and friends probably don't fall into that group. Do they have the life and lifestyle that you want? If they don't, does it make any sense to follow what they do, or pay much heed to their words and expectations? That's what will happen if you spend most of your time around them. Results are an inevitable consequence of actions. So take the same actions as those around you, and you'll get the same results. Einstein defined madness as continuing to do the same things and expecting different results. He was right. Do what they do and you'll get what they've got.

Aside from surrounding yourself physically with people who share your vision, you can use books, DVD's and other media to virtually surround yourself with the same positive influences. The closer you can get to a situation where, you're constantly surrounded and influenced by an enterprise-friendly culture, the more likely that it will become a reality for you.

At first, you'll need to artificially create this environment, but once you start to make progress towards your financial goals, there's no need. Once the process is under way, a strange thing happens – you quickly find yourself surrounded by like-minded folk. When I was penniless, I didn't know a single millionaire. Now I know dozens. I haven't sought them out. They just turned up. And when that happens, your view of what's 'normal' changes for ever.

Just as it's difficult to lose weight if you're surrounded by bloaters who refuse to diet, so it's difficult to make money while you're surrounded by broke people who aren't motivated towards doing anything proactive to change their situation.

Getting what you want often involves making some pretty difficult choices, and this is a big one, because it impacts upon every aspect of your life – social, family and business. The decisions you make here will be critical - not just because they will determine the strength of your enterprises foundations – but also because they will tell you a lot about how committed you really are.

The really good news is that if you are fully committed, the field is wide open for you. Being surrounded by the un-enterprising and the risk averse, starts out as a handicap, but becomes a benefit once it's overcome. The competition is thin on the ground, and it's weak. Once you accept getting rich as the norm, there's not a single thing to stop you doing it.

Health And Safety Rules!

I've been a member of the same gym for a lot more years than I care to remember, and the fact that it still exists is truly astonishing. For reasons that will become abundantly clear, I'm not going to name the place, but I will tell you a little bit about it.

The first thing is the subscription fee - £60 for a full year. Now that might not seem very much to you, but let me tell you that there are long term members who are appalled that it now costs so much. They hark back to the days not so long ago when it was just £25.

I know what you're probably thinking – at a price like that there will be compromises with regard to the standard of facilities on offer, but you'd be wrong. There are no compromises at all. The facilities are consistently and uncompromisingly awful in every conceivable respect.

Take the building (as the wind has almost done on a number of occasions) as a starting point. It's a prefabricated shed type affair with tiny slit windows just below roof height which are impossible to see through. When it rains the roof leaks...badly. You've heard of Aquarobics, well try Aqua-weightlifting. It doesn't work nearly so well. The heating system works beautifully in summer, turning the place into an impromptu sauna, but often gives up altogether in winter. Needless to say there is no air conditioning – an omission that would be less important if the windows opened.

Staffing is another compromise which hasn't been made. Because there are no staff. No manager, no instructors, no receptionists...nothing. When you join you're given a swipe card and someone in a 12ftx12ft office hidden away behind a nearby run down social club tells you where the door is. You're then expected to make your way there and hope to latch on to someone who's been before, and will take pity on you and show you the ropes before you kill yourself.

When you step inside, you'll find that this definitely isn't a health club. Those places have water coolers and hot showers and useable sanitary wear, and this gym has none of those. Attempt to shower here and you're going to come out a lot dirtier than when you went in, and probably with the sort of bacterial infection that will take several doses of antibiotics to fix. I think they had a cleaner once, but he retired just before the millennium. Using the toilets is not something any sane person who values their nether regions would contemplate.

I was going to call it a spit and sawdust place, but that would be only half right. Because there's no sawdust. The fact that there is only one female member (who has far bigger muscles and a deeper voice than me) is indicative of the general ambience of the place. The clientele is almost exclusively made up of young manual workers who walk in off the street in their work clothes, fart, swear and abuse each other a lot, and just get on with it.

The gym floor is covered in a mish-mash of pieces of rubber belting left over from a job one of the members was doing in a factory. None of it meets up or matches, and as a result the floor is uneven. The equipment is in varying states of disrepair. Many of the dumbbells have broken and fractured welds, a number of the machines and benches are unsteady and feel on the brink of collapse and the machine ropes and cables are frequently frayed exposing sharp edges, and with a real danger of them snapping altogether.

There's equipment littered around everywhere. Nobody bothers to put dumbbells or weights back in the racks, and weights are frequently thrown around, dropped and rolled around the room, making taking evasive action a skill you quickly pick up. I don't want you to think these are poncey small weights either. This is a place where you're considered effeminate if you can't handle 100lb dumbbells or bench press a medium sized horse.

So apart from the lack of instruction and supervision, a porous building, health hazard showers and toilets, uneven and slippery floors, dangerously worn equipment and the devil-may-care attitude of the clientele, it's all perfectly safe. If a health and safety officer ever pokes his head around the door, he will close it down in seconds – assuming he doesn't have a heart attack first.

And yet despite all this, I've never known anyone even have cause to reach for a plaster from the first aid box. Which is just as well, because as I'm sure you've probably guessed by now...there is no first aid box.

I was thinking about all this today as I listened to yet another nanny state inspired message on the radio, advising people not to leave the house because of the snow and ice. This is something I don't remember happening until fairly recently. Wind, rain, ice, snow, fog, sunshine, cold and heat all seem to be reasons we should now stay indoors and not make any 'unnecessary journeys' (whatever they are). In fact, unless it's 18 degrees and overcast, it seems that somebody somewhere is determined that we don't go out for fear that we might get 'weathered' in some way.

Just when you thought you were painfully aware of every possible hazard offered up by the British weather, along came Hackney council last year to alert you to something you'd struggle to dream up on your own. Swimmers at the London Fields Lido in the borough were told that they would not be allowed to use the pool if the weather was too wet. They were made to wait outside in a rain shower for fear that it would cloud the water making it difficult for lifeguards to see. So there you have it – too wet to swim.

Does this sort of thing make you angry? I hope that it does because it's just one more example of how we're being patronised and then brain washed into believing and accepting that we can't think, and look out, for ourselves. But of course we can.

Evolution over millions of years has delivered us to this point. That didn't happen without us (and by 'us' I mean our ancestors whose genes we inherit) identifying and dealing with numerous hazards and dangers that were put before us. We didn't need someone else to tell us what to do or how to behave. We assessed the risk, and then made a decision on the most appropriate way to react based on the evidence before us. Our ancestors were good at it. That's why we're here. We are programmed for survival, and don't really need some third party interfering and telling us how to do it.

That probably explains why, despite displaying all the hallmarks of an accident waiting to happen, and having slipped through the health and safety fascists net, my gym hasn't proved to be dangerous in the real world. The people that use it can see and assess the dangers for themselves and adjust their behaviour accordingly. That's what people do when they're not subjected to overbearing control and interference – they exercise self control and look after themselves.

And that's an important point.

You see, once you're brainwashed into thinking that your own safety and survival is someone else's responsibility, there's a very real danger that your own internal survival instincts will wither and die. And if that happens the health and safety fascists will have created the perfect self fulfilling prophecy. They'll have won. They were right. You can't be trusted to look out for yourself after all.

And if you can't be trusted to make decisions on your own safety when you have all the evidence before your eyes to make the right choices, what the heck can you be trusted to do for yourself? If the words and actions of the idiots in charge are anything to go by, not very much at all.

This sort of thing is so insidious, that we stop questioning it after a while. We stop noticing, and that's bad. Self reliance is critical to individual achievement and anything that takes control and responsibility away from us will eat away at that self reliance instinct. And when that happens, it makes achieving our goals just that little bit more difficult.

Stay safe.

How To Tell Lies With Numbers

Monday morning was double maths. I hated Monday mornings. We all did, (apart from Craig Vaughan who was nothing more than a brain on legs) but fortunately we had a plan. And it almost always worked.

You see, Mr Jenkinson our maths teacher was a fanatical fisherman, and so our 'get out of maths strategy' was simple. Someone would casually ask at the start of the lesson. "Did you go fishing at the weekend sir?" and that was it. Half an hour later, he would still be talking about floats, bait and all manner of other tackle I neither knew nor cared about. But what I did care about is that half the lesson had gone without me being fazed by fractions, troubled by trigonometry or agitated by algebra.

Me and maths just didn't get on. It's probably because I couldn't really see the point and nobody explained it to me. An equation was just a collection of letters and numbers with no practical application that I could see. And I could think of no good reason why the angles of a triangle would be of any interest or use to anyone. On the odd occasion where a problem was couched in practical terms, it was usually something along the lines of 'Kevin, Liz, Johnny and Carol have 7 apples, 6 oranges and 12 plums between them. How can they divide them up so each has an equal share, assuming that oranges are worth twice plums, and apples are worth half an orange.' Even this carried no resonance, because the real world answer is that they would simply give up, ditch the fruit, and go and buy some Mars bars and Kit Kats instead.

It is perhaps little surprise therefore that despite attending several months of additional night school lessons (a decision not totally divorced from the fact that I got to sit next to an older girl with a penchant for short skirts and tight tops) I still only managed to scrape a lowly C grade pass at O' level. And even that exceeded everyone's expectations.

For the next few years, I carefully avoided anything maths or number related altogether. It wasn't until I went to university, and was forced to study statistics as part of my course that the light bulb switched on. Numbers could be used for something useful! And if you played your cards right, they might actually help you to make money. Numbers have played a pretty big part in what financial success I've had, ever since.

While I've never quite managed to develop a mathematical brain, I have developed an appreciation of some of the uses and abuses of numbers over the years, and it's the latter which I mainly want to talk about today. You see, if you don't understand numbers, not only can you miss out on some massive opportunities, but you also leave yourself open to being seriously misinformed and misled. I got to thinking about this last night while watching the government's latest alcohol awareness campaign advertisements on TV.

I don't know whether you've seen these latest advertisements. The earlier ones concerned themselves with the dangers of binge drinking, which it has to be said are numerous. But these latest ones are targeting the regular social drinker - the sort of person who drinks a couple of pints or a couple of glasses of wine in an evening. Needless to say, there are dangers in this too, which you haven't even thought about, and to illustrate this, the ad's churn out a catalogue of seemingly worrying statistics.

Now before I go any further, I need to make something very clear. I have no specialist knowledge of the effect of alcohol on the human body. I don't know exactly what effects it has in either the short term or the long term. But if these recent ad's are anything to go by, neither does anyone else. Or if they have, they've got a lousy way of proving it.

In one of the advertisements, aimed at men, a number of claims are made, backed up by official sounding statistics. I don't have the time or space here to go into every one, but I'll just take one of those claims and dissect it. You can do the same thing with any of the 'scary' claims made, and then make your own mind up.

Anyway, here's what the voice over says…

"If you're a man drinking more than two pints of strong lager a day, you're more than 3 times more likely to get mouth cancer."

Now on first hearing, that's pretty worrying isn't it? But what does it really mean?

We'll gloss over the fact that there's no definition of strong lager and get straight to the doomsday quantity of lager quoted… "Over 2 pints per day". How much over 2 pints do we need to drink to kick the 3 times risk into action? If we drink an extra half pint will that do it? And if it will, might we just as well be hung for a sheep as a lamb and have 6 pints because we've already gone over the limit? Is there no difference to the risk between drinking two and a half pints and 10 pints? Surely there must be. And what of the converse situation? If we drink exactly 2 pints a day are we fine? Or do we need to drink one and three quarters? I think we should be told.

But moving back one stage, there's something else that isn't explained at all. Assuming that we do drink 'over two pints' of strong lager, whom are we more than three times as likely to get mouth cancer than? Is it the bloke who drinks nothing at all, or the bloke who drinks one pint a day or the one who drinks exactly two pints? Or is it someone else?

We have no way of knowing. Nothing is defined, nothing is nailed down. It would be bad enough coming from some dodgy double glazing firm, but this is supposed to be our government conveying a very important health message. And it gets worse.

Let's cut them a bit of slack and assume that on average, men who drink more than two pints of strong lager have a higher incidence of mouth cancer than lighter drinkers. Does this therefore mean that the lager has led directly to the mouth cancer? Of course it doesn't. Heavier drinkers are also more likely to make other lifestyle choices which may not be particularly healthy. People rarely make 'bad' choices in isolation. They're certainly more likely to be smokers, and as anyone who's ever over-indulged in alcohol will testify, far more likely to eat the sort of greasy, fat laden slop (yes, I speak of you, Doner Kebab!) which sober folk tend to stay well clear of. It is no coincidence that fast food outlets are usually clustered around pubs.

So if there is this higher incidence of mouth cancer, is it not just as likely that smoking or diet may be to blame, or certainly things that acts in tandem with alcohol as contributory factors? Multiple factors like these are notoriously difficult to screen out and weight statistically. They rely on building a detailed, accurate and truthful picture of an   individual's lifestyle which those individuals are not always willing or able to give.

And now we turn to the stomach churning statistic, 'three times as likely'...three times! For this purpose, let's assume that alcohol is totally to blame, 2 pints is the limit, and any more and you've trebled your risk of mouth cancer. What does that actually mean? Well, when taken in isolation, not very much. If one in ten people normally get mouth cancer, then trebling your risk to three in ten....30%...is worrying indeed. On the other hand, if one person in a million normally gets it, then trebling the risk to three in a million isn't nearly so scary. So the only way we can read anything into this figure is to know the underlying incidence of mouth cancer. Of course, the ads don't tell us.

So I looked it up, and about 9 people in every 100,000 fall victim to oral cancer each year. If we're assuming that this includes all those people who are drinking beyond their two pints a day, then the underlying rate (for light/none drinkers) must be somewhere around 5 people in every thousand. It therefore follows that heavier drinkers will have an incidence somewhere around the 15 per 100,000 mark.

The extra drinking has given them ten extra chances in a hundred thousand of getting the disease each year...or put another way, an extra one in 10,000 chance. So there are at least two 'factual' ways of stating the same information:

1. Drinking more than two pints of strong lager each day makes you three times more likely to get mouth cancer.

2. Drinking more than two pints of strong lager each day, gives you an annual extra 1 in 10,000 chance that you will get mouth cancer.

How you perceive and react to these two statements will be down to you as an individual, but I doubt there are many that would perceive and react to them in exactly the same way. The information has been presented in a way that fits in with the objectives of the people who created it. Statement No.1 may be factually correct, (although, as we've seen, that is in doubt) but I think a lot of people would see it as misleading in the context of statement No.2.

Disraeli is reported to have said that, "There are three kinds of lies: lies, damned lies, and statistics." Well over a century later, his successors are still taking full advantage of the fact.

There's a growing tendency for information to be presented in easy to digest sound bites. People are busy; they don't have time to take in huge swathes of information on the multifarious topics they're expected to be up to date on these days. And that plays right into the hands of the persuaders who use statistics to shape thinking, behaviour and actions.

My purpose here isn't to persuade you on the rights and wrongs of the alcohol/health debate. The truth is that I'm in the dark just as much as anyone else. No my real purpose is to get you to take a critical look at any statistics you're presented with, and ask yourself a few vital questions:

1. Where do the statistics come from?

2. Are there vested interests at stake?

3. Are the key factors properly defined?

4. Are there other factors involved which could affect or create the result?

5. What are the real numbers behind the headline figures and percentages quoted?

When you do this, you give yourself a far stronger and more rational basis for the decisions you make, than if you allow yourself to be side-tracked by a wave of statistical misdirection. Plus of course, you get the added satisfaction of knowing that the smart-arsed, controlling and power obsessed politicians have failed to channel you down the alley that suits them best. And there are few better reasons for doing anything than that.

I don't think this chapter would be complete though, without encouraging you to consider the implication of flipping the coin – turning from gamekeeper to poacher. These government advertisements have been carefully crafted to create a perception. They do not tell lies, but they do use the presentation of statistics to shape thoughts, behaviour and actions in a particular direction.

So what about your business…what about the areas in your life you're looking to have an influence? You can be sure that there will be relevant numbers and statistics available; you can be sure that there will be more than one way in which they can be presented…and you can also be sure that one of those ways will be more helpful to you in achieving your goals than the others.

Whether you choose to use it will be as much a moral decision, as one based on pure business logic.

Michael McIntyre And The Debt Collectors

I'm disappointed. I used to be a fan of comedian Michael McIntyre, but he just went right down in my estimation.

A couple of weeks ago he was contracted to appear at a private function for financial services company, Cabot Financial for a fee of £28,000. But an hour before the event, he pulled out on a matter of 'principle' – because he discovered that the company operate in the field of debt collection.

Cabot takes over the bad debts incurred by credit card companies and banks, and it was this that McIntyre objected to. You see, before he hit the big time (and made a multi million pound fortune) about 3 years ago, it turns out that he was over £40,000 in debt, owing money to banks and credit card companies and barely able to pay the rent.

I think it's a mark of much of what is wrong in the UK at the moment that Macintye's withdrawal was widely perceived by the public to be honourable and heroic, and that Cabot were painted as the villains of the piece. Aside from the most obvious reason why this was a dishonourable act – McIntyre had signed up to do something, and it was up to him to fully acquaint himself with the details before doing that – there's a much bigger issue here.

When McIntyre got himself into £40,000 of debt, it probably didn't happen by accident. Nor did it happen overnight. What probably happened is that he made a decision to live beyond his financial means. He chose to use other people's money to finance a lifestyle that his earning power at the time could not support. He made the decision to use credit to pay for stuff he wanted to buy – stuff that other people in similar financial circumstances chose to forego. Lots of people do this, and while it's not the way I'd choose to live, each to their own, and it's fine for people who can manage the debt.

But some folk, who run up debts like this, aren't willing or able to repay them. When that happens, they frequently come up against a company of debt collectors like Cabot. And what's wrong with that? These aren't Neanderthal thugs who come knocking on your door at midnight with a baseball bat. They are professional debt collectors who go about recovering monies owed to their clients by the due legal process.

So who's the real dishonourable party here - the debt collection company attempting to get back what people have borrowed, but can't or won't pay back - or the borrowers themselves who have had the benefit of the money they've borrowed but are now attempting to escape paying the price?

If you had to trust someone in a financial matter, who would it be - the bloke who borrowed some money but didn't pay it back, or the bloke trying to get his money back after lending it out to a defaulting debtor?

Not a hard question to answer is it? So why did so many people sympathise with McIntyres stance when he pulled out of that engagement with Cabot? The answer reveals much about the way the national psyche has changed in recent years, and explains why the vast majority of people find themselves handicapped by their attitude.

For every Michael McIntyre, going from £40,000 in debt to multi millionaire status, there are tens of thousands of others who do not. It's fortunate that McIntyre has a unique talent, because this sort of attitude makes it difficult to succeed via a more mainstream route. The subtext of his decision to pull out of that engagement seems to be this...

When people get into financial difficulties, it's not a situation of their own making. The bank either lent them too much money, or they have run into difficulties they didn't foresee. It isn't ethical or fair to push those people to make every reasonable effort to abide by the agreement they entered into. Someone else is to blame and someone else should pay.

How else can you possibly justify taking the moral high ground against debt collectors attempting to enforce what was freely and openly agreed? How else can you justify siding with the man who has spent money that doesn't belong to him, and isn't able to pay it back?

Now I know that a lot of people will say "Yeah, but no but yeah…." In a Vicky Pollardesque sort of way before arguing that this money is borrowed from banks, credit card companies and other large financial institutions that have massive resources and can afford to bear the loss. At the risk of insulting their intelligence, I would ask those people where they think these huge financial institutions get their money from, and who they think pays for these unpaid debts, in the end?

Just in case asking such a question wouldn't be insulting their intelligence after all, let me spell out the answer here. The cost of bad debts doesn't rest with the banks and other financial institutions. They're far too canny for that. Ultimately it finds its way to the door of prudent and honest borrowers through higher interest rates on their loans, and careful savers, through lower interest rates on their deposits.

Next time you hear someone cheering on a debtor keeping one step ahead of the debt collectors, perhaps you might point that out to them.

But here's the main point I want to make…

If you find yourself siding with defaulting debtors over their creditors, then it's a fairly strong indication that you are going to find success and achievement something of a struggle. Success almost always requires that you take full responsibility for your actions and the consequences of those actions. And as a result, you expect the same in others. It requires that you assess the risks associated with any action you're going to take, and fully accept the blame if things don't work out. Because when you leave yourself the escape route of having someone else to blame for failure, it's pretty easy to take it - and allow yourself to fail.

If you take full responsibility in advance though – resolve to take the consequences of a failure squarely on the chin - the chances of success in any endeavour you undertake, are multiplied many times over.

None of this is easy of course. Taking responsibility is onerous and painful. Sometimes it can result in a massive blow to the ego –

as well as the bank balance. But it's the only proven and workable way forward. You see, if it was easy, everyone would be doing it. If everyone was doing it, it wouldn't give you a massive advantage. And if you didn't have a massive advantage, you'd be hidden away, back in the pack, with the also-rans...

And I'm pretty sure that's not where you want to be.

Simon Cowell's Birthday Party

It was Simon Cowell's 50th birthday this week and he had a little party. The party was reported to have cost £1 Million and Cowell came in for a barrage of criticism for what was seen as 'excess' in times of economic difficulty. He was lambasted for spending so much on a party when so many people are struggling to make ends meet.

I've known for a long time now, that the vast majority of the population understand little or nothing about money, and this sort of criticism is proof of that. The implication is that money is somehow 'wasted' or 'used up' when it's spent. So when Simon Cowell spends £50,000 on limousines to get guests to his party or £40,000 for flowers, this money somehow disappears and is no longer available to be used by other people but that's not what happens at all. In fact the reverse is true.

To stick to the limousine example for a moment, the £50,000 goes into the bank account of the car hire companies, one of whom we'll call Nigel's Cars. Nigel in turn pays his suppliers and employees. One of those employees is Jack, a driver and one of the lowest paid workers in the economy. If Cowell hadn't thrown the party, Jack wouldn't have had any work that night.

That would have been a shame because the money he was paid for transporting guests to Simon Cowell's party funded a meal in Luigi's Italian restaurant the following evening with his wife. The price of the meal went partly into the hands of Luigi, who in turn paid his suppliers, and some of it went to the waiter, Mario – again one of the lowest paid workers in the economy.

If Cowell hadn't thrown his party, and hired Nigel's firm who paid Jack, who paid Luigi, who in turn paid Mario, that would have been disappointing for Mario, because he would have missed out on the £5 tip that Jack gave him. And in turn, Imran the local newsagent would have missed out, because that's where Mario spent his tip on a Health and Fitness magazine. Imran wasn't in the shop that day though. Mario was served by a shop assistant called Carol. She's on the minimum wage, but Imran can only afford to pay her at all if people like Mario come in and buy magazines. If that stopped, he'd have to make her redundant and then she'd need to start claiming benefits.

Can you see what's happening here? The cash is going from one wealthy guy and cascading down through the economy, creating income and jobs for scores of other people on its path – and incidentally tax revenue for the government, while cutting the social security bill. This is just one tiny strand of the cash cascade that flowed from that party. Just within the confines of limo hire, there would have been dozens of Nigel's, Jack's Luigi's Mario's, Imran's and Carols'. Scale that up to include all the products and services needed to run a £1 Million party, and the economic impact is vast and practically incalculable.

So what's going on here - why the criticism? Well aside from economic ignorance, there's something else – something that would probably ensure that the criticism remained long after the economic ignorance had been removed. Envy and jealousy.

What the critics see is a rich and famous guy and his rich and famous friends enjoying a party they're not invited to. They see them enjoying expensive food, wine and entertainment that they can't afford. And they don't like it. So rather than use the event as a stimulus and motivation for their own enhanced achievement, (I'll have that one day) they seek to destroy (It's not right that he should have it).

This is the response of the idle and feckless of course. It's far easier to say that someone else should have the spoils of their success taken away than it is to commit to emulating their success. And as I hope I've demonstrated, there is absolutely no shame or harm in a wealthy individual liberally spending his or her own money. In fact there is only a positive benefit for the economy and population as a whole.

This negative attitude to wealth would be bad enough were it confined to uneducated and underachieving individuals, of whom perhaps no more can be expected, but it goes much further than that. In fact it goes right to the very top of our government - to people whose education and experience must surely have directed them to the truth of the matter, but who still choose to act at variance with it.

The top rate of income tax has now been raised to 50%, ostensibly to help plug the fiscal deficit. But even the most optimistic estimates suggest it will have virtually no significant effect, and the most likely outcome is far, far worse than that.

Just yesterday I had a meeting with a top firm of accountants who confirmed what I already instinctively knew - the increase is unlikely to put any extra cash into the government coffers. Many of the rich and powerful individuals who this affects can choose to live anywhere in the world. Is it any surprise that significant numbers of them will choose to live in a country which doesn't take over half their income?

And those that stay – will they just grin and bear it? No they won't. Some will enter into complex arrangements to remove swathes of their income from the tax net (the accountants were working on legal schemes within minutes of the rise being announced) and others will simply cut back on their work to stay within the old tax bands.

The end result will be net reduction in the tax collected, an exodus of movers and shakers from the country, and a fall in demand, spending and hence employment. The disgraceful thing is that the people who instigated this change are educated and experienced enough to know exactly what will happen. They do know, but like the people criticising Simon Cowell, they are more concerned with removing perceived inequality, than they are with creating a net benefit for society as a whole.

It's called the politics of envy. And unfortunately, it's alive, well and fighting fit in 2010. With the new government committed to standing by the new rate (chiefly I suspect because they think that what I've just explained in a few sentences is too hard for the electorate to grasp) the error will be compounded, and the (ideologically sane but economically senseless) policy will be perpetuated.

I know what you're thinking – the sooner I'm swept to power in a bloodless military coup, the better. And you're quite right. Reckon I'll have Simon Cowell as my Chancellor. Apparently he's got all the money.

John's Guide To Farming

If you've ever visited the beautiful city of Edinburgh, I'd be prepared to bet you've also visited its castle. Most visitors do. It's one of the most photographed buildings in the UK, and famous around the world. It's on the 'tick-off' list of every self respecting American, Australian or Japanese tourist.

So would it surprise you to learn that 20% of people living in Edinburgh have never visited it? It doesn't really surprise me…and it's not   because the Scots are too tight to pay the entrance fee. That's a crude and unfair regional stereotype about meanness, which as a Yorkshireman, I'm very keen to discourage.

If I look out of the window right in front of where I'm writing this now, I can see The Magna Science and Adventure Centre. Whilst it's not quite on a par with Edinburgh Castle, it is one of the most popular tourist destinations in the North of England. And yet less than half the people in our office have ever visited it. They could walk there, and yet more have visited Alton Towers than the attraction literally on their doorstep.

So what's going on here?

Between 1900 and 1925 a gentleman by the name of Russell Conwell delivered the same iconic speech around 5,000 times. And the fact that 20% of Edinburgh residents haven't visited the castle, 50% of my staff haven't visited Magna (and someone sitting six feet from me right now has been to most corners of Europe, America and the far East, but has never visited the Yorkshire Dales) suggests that the message he delivered in that speech is as relevant today as it was back then. What's more, it's a message that could be the key that unlocks a number of financial, psychological and social treasure chests for you.

Conwell's speech centred around the apparently true story of a north African farmer who became frustrated by the poor living he was making. He heard tales of how other farmers had made millions by going out and discovering diamond mines, and got very excited by them. In fact he became so excited that he couldn't wait to sell his farm and go out prospecting on his own account.

With the farm hastily sold off, he set off to travel the African continent, searching for those elusive diamonds in one place after another. He had no success, and several years later, tired, beaten and disillusioned, he threw himself in a river one day and drowned.

Meanwhile, things were going a little better for the man who bought the farm. He was walking across his land one day when he spotted an attractive blue and red rock on the bed of a small stream. He didn't know what it was, but liked the look of it and so picked it up, took it home and placed it on his mantel as an ornament.

A few weeks later, a visitor to the farm picked up the rock and almost fainted. He asked the owner if he knew what it was. He didn't. The visitor told him that it was a huge rough diamond…the largest ever discovered - a fact that was of intense interest to the owner as there were hundreds of similar stones in the stream. The farm which the original owner abandoned in search of diamonds turned out to be the source of one of the largest diamond mines in the whole of Africa.

I'm sure you can see what pulls all this together. The human psyche default position seems to tend towards attempting to fulfil wants, needs and aspirations externally. The unwritten, underlying subtext is clear…the answers to our needs and problems are to be found far away. They can't possibly be close or we would already be benefiting from them. I can't pretend to understand the psychology of this…something to do with taking for granted what we have and over-valuing what others have perhaps…but whatever is behind it, it creates it's own reality.

So what's to be done about it? Well let's stick with the farm analogy for a moment. Your farm might be a business, a job, a relationship, a house or something else that's important to you. Heck, it might even *be* a farm!

Have you really had a good look around your farm recently? Do you know everything that's there? Might there be undiscovered diamonds laying hidden in areas you haven't recently explored? Might the diamonds be 'in the rough' and difficult to spot at first? Do you know anyone who might be able to help identify and then polish these rough diamonds? Do other farms only look good from a distance? Might the diamonds in other farms be just as difficult to harvest once you get there?

The truth is that when you see other folk flashing off their diamonds, they don't necessarily have a better farm than you. But what they've learned to do is:

1. Search their farm properly
2. Recognise what rough diamonds look like
3. Polish these rough diamonds effectively.

You see, it's only when you've done all this that it sense to move off the farm.

Just to focus on business and money making for a moment, you almost certainly have some tremendous opportunities right at your feet. If you haven't found them yet it may be because you're too busy looking further afield or don't know what they look like in their raw state. Just as a diamond doesn't look like the glistening jewel you see adorning a piece of jewellery, when it comes out of the ground, so a 'hot' opportunity doesn't look anything like the finished product in the raw state.

Every one of us is sitting on our own personal 'field of diamonds'. No two are exactly the same. Your 'field' boundaries are determined by your knowledge, skills, experience, contacts, strengths, weaknesses, interests and preferences. And the great thing is that to mine this field, you don't have to go anywhere. Because the excavation tool you need is located right between your ears.

Morgan Freeman And The Mexican

Hollywood legend Morgan Freeman didn't always want to be an actor. As a young black man growing up in the southern states of America in the 1950's, you can imagine that he wasn't starting out with the best of advantages. But that didn't deter him, because what he wanted more than anything else, was to become a fighter pilot.

He joined the US airforce at age 16 as an engineer, and studied and worked hard until finally, at age 21, he was given the opportunity he'd dreamed of for so long – to train as a pilot. Given the prejudice and barriers in place at that time, this must have been an incredible achievement. But as he sat in the cockpit of the plane for the first time, a transformation came over him. A fundamental change took place. This wasn't what he wanted at all.

Freeman realised that he was sitting in a machine designed specifically to kill and destroy. That would be his job – his role in life. And that wasn't the idea he's fallen in love with. What Freeman had fallen in love with was some Hollwoodesque notion of what a fighter pilot was and represented – how they were seen, perceived and treated. He wanted to play the role of a fighter pilot, but without having to do what a fighter pilot does.

He walked out on the air force that same day and never went back.

Here's another story. I suspect this one isn't true, but it further illustrates the point I'm hoping to make…

A boat docked in a tiny Mexican village. An American tourist complimented the Mexican fisherman on the quality of his catch.

"How long did it take you to get those?" he asked.

"Not so long," said the Mexican.

"Then why didn't you stay out longer and catch more?" asked the American.

The Mexican explained that his small catch was quite enough to meet his needs and feed his family.

"So what do you do with the rest of your time?" asked the American.

"I sleep late, fish a little, play with my children, and take a siesta with my wife. In the evening, I go into the village to see my friends, have a few drinks, play the guitar and sing a few songs. I have a full life."

The American interrupted. "I have an MBA from Harvard and I can help you! You should start by fishing longer every day. You can then sell the extra fish you catch. With the extra revenue, you can buy a bigger boat."

"And after that?" asked the Mexican.

"With the extra money the bigger boat will bring, you can buy a second boat and then a third boat, and then more until you have an entire fleet of trawlers. Instead of selling your fish to a middle man, you can then negotiate directly with the processing plants. Pretty soon you could open your own plant. You could leave this little village and move to Mexico City, Los Angeles, or even New York! From there you could direct your whole enterprise."

"How long would that take?" asked the Mexican.

"Twenty — perhaps twenty-five years," replied the American.

"And after that?"

"Afterwards? Well, my friend," laughed the American, "that's when it gets really interesting. When your business gets really big, you can start selling stocks and make millions!"

"Millions? Really? And after that?" said the Mexican.

"After that you'll be able to retire, live in a beautiful place near the coast, sleep late, play with your children, catch a few fish, take siestas with your wife and spend your evenings drinking and enjoying your friends."

We all have goals and aspirations. We often spend years dreaming about them and working towards them, but without giving a great deal of thought to the key questions…

Why do I want this? Do I REALLY want this? These are uncomfortable questions because they get right to the heart of who we are, what really motives us, and what we really want out of life.

Morgan Freeman discovered that he didn't really want to be a fighter pilot…he'd just bought into a myth about what a pilot was, and wanted the status, prestige and standing that a pilot enjoyed. The Mexican fisherman realised what the American tourist couldn't yet see – that he already had what great wealth would bring – the time and freedom to live exactly as he pleased. He didn't need to invest the 20 years of blood, sweat and tears to become wealthy to get the benefits he wanted.

So what about you?

What are you dreaming about or working towards? If it's a particular business or career, do you really want to go into that business or career? Or when you think deeply about it, are you doing it to garner some ancillary social or financial benefits that you feel will come with it. And if that's the case, is there some (perhaps easier or more palatable) way you can enjoy these same benefits without spending a huge portion of your irreplaceable life working towards something you don't really want?

Morgan Freeman discovered his outlet through acting. The Mexican fisherman was smart enough to realise that he already had what he wanted. Very few people do this – unless they happen to be apocryphal characters, created to make an important point!

So again, what about you?

What do you really want? Is it at the top of the ladder you're currently climbing? And even if it is, might there be another ladder somewhere else which gets you exactly where you want to be without the steep climb or the feeling of vertigo when you get to the top?

These are questions that only you can answer, but I hope I've at least given you a reason to ask them.

Inventing The Perfect Parachute

I want to tell you the tale of Billy Blunderbuss and Tommy Treadright. Both were aspiring parachute designers and both thought they had a winning idea for a new improved parachute.

Now I know what you're probably thinking....these are not real people and are in fact fictitious characters with silly names chosen for their comedic value. Perish the very thought. Billy and Tommy are as real as they need to be and have a great deal to teach us.

Billy is (or should I say was) true to his name and a bit of a Blunderbuss. When he had an idea, he wanted to get on with things. He was a man to 'go for it'. So when he came up with his parachute idea, he drew it out on a scrap of paper and then spent every waking moment for over a year, making a full sized prototype. It looked great and he was confident, so he hired a small plane, instructed the pilot to fly to 5,000 feet and jumped out with the parachute strapped to his back.

Who knows what went through his mind as he pulled the ripcord and it came off in his hand, but it couldn't have been good. Billy plummeted to the ground and made such a hole that they couldn't decide whether to dig him out, or just fill it in and put a stone on top. By any measure, things hadn't gone well.

Now Tommy took a different approach. He drew out his parachute on paper and then entered the characteristics into an aerodynamics programme on his computer. The programme quickly flagged up that the parachute wouldn't work in its current form, so Tommy redesigned it. The programme now suggested that the parachute could work in principle and so Tommy created a small scale model of it. He attached the parachute to a weight and threw it off a stepladder.

The model worked reasonably well but the descent was far too fast. In real life, anyone using it would probably break their legs. Tommy made some adjustments, and over a period of weeks, honed his design so that eventually the descent was about right.

Heartened by this, Tommy hired the same aircraft Billy had used before. The pilot, still traumatised from hearing Billy's screams as he plunged to the ground, was relieved to learn that Tommy had no intention of jumping out of the plane yet. He'd made a life sized dummy which he intended to hurl out at 5,000 feet. They both watched as the parachute opened but then got blown out of shape as the wind got hold of it and caused it to malfunction. The model crashed to earth at around 30mph and was smashed to pieces.

Undeterred, Tommy went back to the drawing board, and made another prototype, and then another and then another, as each was put to the same test and found wanting. But he didn't give up, and eventually, he arrived at a design that seemed to work perfectly. It was ready for a full live human test...a test which Tommy didn't carry out himself. After all, if there WAS a problem, he needed to be around to put it right.

As his 'test jumper' floated serenely to the ground, Tommy breathed a sigh of relief. It had been a long road, but he'd got there in the end.

Success!

But this chapter isn't about success. It's actually about failure. So let me ask you this...who's the biggest failure in this story, Billy Blunderbuss or Tommy Treadright, and what does that tell us about the nature of failure? Before you answer I want to make a confession...

I may have given you the impression that I'm a succcss, but if success and failure are at the opposite ends of the spectrum, I'm not sure that description is either fair or accurate. You see, although I have many of the things that people associate with success, I have to admit that I've also had (and continue to have) more than my fair share of failures. If someone looking at you and I from the outside were to judge me to be more successful than you, I'd be prepared to bet that I fail more often than you do. And if that same person were to judge you more successful than me, then there's every chance that you have more failures than I do.

Isn't that strange and counter-intuitive? The more successful you are, the more failure you're likely to experience.

So going back to our friends Billy and Tommy, who's the biggest failure? Well, in terms of sheer volume of failures it has to be Tommy. His computer model failed, and his scale model failed several times, as did his full sized model. Billy only failed the once. But Tommy ultimately succeeded and Billy didn't. Billy's failure was a big one.

Over the years, much of the correspondence I've received from people desperate for success has focussed on failure…experiences of it, fear of it, and their desperation to avoid it. And when these people talk of failure, they are usually referring to the sort experienced by Billy Blunderbuss…Total, complete and final. But what Tommy Treadright teaches us is that there's another kind of failure which isn't nearly so negative. It's failure which is planned, controlled, limited in scope and if managed properly, can ultimately lead you towards success rather than away from it.

Almost all major success is preceded by small failures. So the goal isn't to avoid failures altogether, but rather to manage the scale and nature of them so that they move us closer to where we want to be, and aren't so catastrophic that the big prize is lost altogether. I think it's a misunderstanding about this that causes more enterprises to wither and die at birth, than anything else…

Because if you're dead set on avoiding failure at all costs, the safest thing to do is…nothing!

And when you do nothing, you don't fail, but you don't succeed either.

Something you may not know about me is that I have a totally unblemished record in the boxing ring. I have never been beaten. I have never failed once. But the absence of any Lonsdale belts or a bank account stuffed with prize money - the spoils of success – tell the other side of the story. I have never tried. Not failing and succeeding are not the same thing.

At least Billy Blunderbuss didn't fall in to the trap of doing nothing, but his approach was still fatally (literally!) flawed. He set himself up to fail big, and that's what most people do. And to make matters worse, they usually set themselves up to fail slowly as well.

Failing big is bad. Failing slowly is bad. Failing big and slow is the worst combination of all. Sadly, this is something that happens all the time...

The would-be entrepreneur puts plans in motion for a massive all or nothing launch of their concept, product or business. Because the launch is going to be massive, it's going to take a lot of money and time to get to the point of 'take-off'. The success or failure of the entire enterprise rests on this one all or nothing event. If it fails, it's a catastrophic failure of Blunderbuss proportions....

All the money is gone. The time is gone. There's no way back.

The solution is to structure your approach so that when you fail, (and you almost certainly will at some point) you fail small and you fail quickly. Small and quick failures become minor correction points on the road to success rather than the Armageddon scenario which is characteristic of their large and slow counterparts. Anyone can fail big and slow, but it takes careful planning, and an acute awareness of the steps you need to take to reach a goal, to fail quickly and fail small.

The idea of aiming to fail fast and small will probably not mean the same in your business as it does in mine, but it's worth investing some time and effort figuring out exactly what it does mean. While Tommy Treadright is enjoying the spoils of his success, Billy Blunderbuss is languishing six foot under without anyone having to call on the services of a doctor or a gravedigger.

They both tried, they both failed. But I know which one I'd rather be.

The Ship's Funnel

As a man, there are certain things, you'd feel a little embarrassed owning up to – crying during Bambi for example, or having a penchant for wearing ladies underwear. Included in that list would be getting seasick on a Pedalo. While I'm making no admissions with regard to the first two (maybe another day) I will own up here and now to the third. A long time has passed and the wounds have almost healed.

It was 1987 and marginally off the coast of St Julians Bay in Malta. In my defence, I have to say that it was a bit choppy and the previous night's Pina Colada was already making overtures regarding a re-appearance when I got on board. But there's no doubt that it does little for your macho image or street cred, to be forced to abandon ship (and your girlfriend) 100 yards out and swim back to shore, for fear of having a long pedal back while picking regurgitated coconut out of your sandals.

I only mention this, to give you some idea of my state of mind when it was recently suggested that we might go on a cruise. Me and water just don't get on. I'm fine when I'm in it – just not so good when I'm on it. A recent awkward moment in a rowing boat on a glass-smooth boating lake in Cleethorpes confirmed that my constitution hasn't exactly improved with age.

I consulted numerous cruise veterans, all of whom assured me that I wouldn't even know that the ship was moving. I trusted these people. And so imagine my confusion last Tuesday, with the cruise duly booked and embarked upon, when I awoke at 2.00am to find the ship being tossed around like a cork, and to hear the sort of crunching, grinding and juddering noises I'd imagine they experienced just before the Titanic disappeared below the waves.

This went on for what seemed like hours – but miraculously I wasn't ill.

Early next morning, I woke to the dulcet tones of the Captain, booming out over the ships tanoy. Apparently we'd sailed through a force eleven storm the previous night, but the ship had coped "very well". You could have fooled me! He was probably right though.

When I looked it up, I found out that a force eleven storm equates to 50ft waves and the only thing worse is a force twelve - which is a hurricane. Just the thing for someone without sealegs. But I was fine.

It was to take transport of a different kind to give my stomach a proper test.

The night after the storm, we arrived in La Palma, which is one of the lesser-known Canary Islands, and has the distinction of being the steepest island in the world. It's somewhere we'd never been before and knew nothing about. So I did what I'd never do under normal circumstances – I booked a coach tour.

Now don't get me wrong, I have nothing against coaches – for other people. There's no finer conveyance for transporting school children, pensioners and the mentally impaired - professional footballers for example. But they fall fairly and squarely into the category of 'public transport'…something that just doesn't fit with my need to be in full control at all times. I'd already had to relinquish more control than I was comfortable with, by allowing someone else to steer the ship. I feared this coach malarkey may be a step too far. But it was too late now. It was parked in front of the ship and one of the seats had my name on it.

We got on board, and my wife and daughter took the two seats in front of me. I was joined by a lady with a name badge and a clipboard. A sly glance to my right confirmed that she worked for the cruise line and was doing a quality assessment on the trip. I'd love to know what she wrote, I really would.

It all started well enough. The tour guide was a blonde haired, middle aged woman from Leicester called Diane. I'd imagine she went to La Palma on holiday in 1983, met a swarthy lothario called Raul, and never went home again. But then again, I imagine lots of things. Anyway, the coach set off and Diane waxed lyrical about the wonderful flora, fauna and wildlife we were about to witness in the National Park, located high up in the centre of the island. We were definitely in the right place she told us – far better than any of the other islands. I was getting quite excited. That's a lie. I never get excited. But I was starting to think the day might not turn into a total disaster, which is my normal default position on such occasions.

After about 40 minutes of enthusiastic build up, we passed the park visitor centre on our right, which Diane told us we regrettably wouldn't have time to visit. I couldn't help noticing it was getting quite windy by this point, but thought nothing of it. A couple of minutes later, we arrived at a barrier at the entrance to the park, and Diane leaned out to have a conversation with a park ranger.

"I don't know whether you caught that", she said (How the heck would I? They were speaking Spanish) "but the park is closed today because of the wind". An entire national park closed because of wind! Imagine closing the Peak District or Dartmoor because of wind – or anything else. Incredible.

Someone asked about Plan B, and a somewhat flustered Diane admitted she had no Plan B, but would ring Pablo in the office for instructions. Pablo wasn't answering his phone – probably out watching a bullfight or seducing a teenage holidaymaker from Crewe called Tracey – but in any event, we were driven to the visitor's centre, while he was located and dragged back to work.

What a dump! It turned out to be a dark concrete monstrosity hidden behind a building site. Its only redeeming feature was that it had toilets. Unfortunately, they were the kind of toilets often found in foreign parts, where the urinals are in full view of anyone walking past. This wouldn't have been such a problem if people had been walking past - but they weren't. They were standing right outside, queuing for the Ladies.

This would have been less of a problem if the folk in the queue were strangers I'd never see again, rather than people I was about to share a coach with for the next two hours, and a ship for the next two weeks. If someone catches you mid-flow, you just don't want to set eyes on them again. You really don't.

I clambered dispirited and humiliated, back on the coach to be informed that Pablo had now been contacted (maybe Tracey had given him the knock-back) and a revised itinerary had been worked out. I don't know exactly what he said, but from what followed can only assume that it was something like "Drive them around for a bit and waffle."

We were each handed a leaflet, describing what we would have seen if we'd been let into the park (talk about rubbing it in) and for the next 45 minutes were driven through some of the most God forsaken villages and countryside I think I've seen anywhere, while Diane rambled on about what we could have experienced - if only the weather had been better or if it was a different day or if it was a different time of year.

Apparently anything and everything of any interest or importance happened, appeared, or could have been experienced on another day. But not today. All there was today was bananas...acres of bloody bananas.

Now you won't catch me bad-mouthing bananas. It's the perfect healthy and handy snack food. I eat them most days. But when you've seen one banana field, you've seen them all, and there's a limit to the amount of information you can take in about bananas, without developing an almost irresistible urge to use one as an impromptu gag. Diane was fascinated by bananas. Maybe living in a place like this gets you that way. But I wasn't, and I suspect from the glum faces of my fellow passengers, neither were they.

By this stage the lady next to me, who was supposed to be assessing the trip, had fallen asleep. Which is a shame, because she missed the most exciting part?

The coach driver took a phone call. He mumbled something to Diane in Spanish, and I noticed a discernible change in his driving. We were travelling along very narrow, twisty, country roads with steep sheer drops just inches away, but he was driving rather quickly now. Too quickly. Ever wondered whether it's possible to powerslide a coach? I can tell you that it is.

Diane continued with her droning lecture about bananas, (If I'm feeling particularly vitriolic towards you one day, I'll educate you on the differences between the La Palma banana and its Caribbean cousin) while the woman two seats in front started to go a rather fetching shade of green. I wasn't feeling too good myself by this point – far worse in fact, than in the force eleven storm the previous evening. Every now and then, the driver would take another phone call, mumble something else in Spanish, and push his foot just that little bit further to the boards.

Eventually, after about 15 minutes of this mayhem, Diane came clean...

"Erm, you may have noticed that we aren't travelling at our normal leisurely pace, (Oh really?) But the thing is that they're closing the road ahead of us at 11.00 o'clock for essential roadworks and if we don't get there for then, we'll be stuck."

The thought of being trapped on this damned coach on this damned island for a minute longer than necessary caused me to abandon all thoughts of personal safety and to mentally implore the driver to give it some more welly. At 2 minutes to eleven, and with my breakfast almost at the point of no return (or should that be some return?) we passed the cut off point, and everything returned to normal.

On another day, at a different time of year, in different weather and without road works, La Palma may be a wonderful place. But today it was crap beyond measure.

To cap things off, Diane announced that we would stop for refreshments, before returning to the ship. I was temporarily buoyed at the prospect of a cold beer, but my hopes were quickly dashed.

"There will be coffee and tea", she said. "Now I wouldn't drink the coffee at all, if I was you. As for the tea, well I'm a tea drinker, and can drink it anywhere, but you might not find the tea here...err... to your taste. It's not very strong and erm...not very warm either."

All of this was delivered without any sense of irony or humour. I turned to sleeping beauty sitting next to me who'd woken up by now "It's alright for you," I said "you're getting paid to be here." She said nothing.

We arrived in a village so devoid of life that even the tumbleweed couldn't be arsed to tumble, and just lay lifeless by the side of the road. Diane pointed out a miserable looking, utilitarian and characterless village hall, where we were instructed to queue up for the aforementioned maligned beverages and a biscuit. I had water.

I looked around the room. I don't think I've seen such a sea of uniformly miserable faces, outside of a crematorium. But by this time, me my wife and daughter were virtually hysterical with laughter. The whole thing was just so bad beyond belief, that it was funny. I'm not sure anyone else was in on the joke though.

As we returned to the coach, the green woman had returned to a more healthy yellow, and she thanked us for taking her mind off the worst excesses of the Coach Grand Prix by making her laugh. I didn't know she'd been listening. The rest of the journey back to the ship was punctuated by more bananas, more tales of interesting things that happen on La Palma when we're not there, and a frankly astonishing request for a round of applause for the driver. If it had been down to me, he'd have been deafened by the silence, and Googling 'gearstick orifice extraction techniques' on his return to the depot, but Brits are remarkably polite at such times, and most complied.

I was just starting to feel very sick again when the ship mercifully loomed into view. We got off the coach in surprisingly high spirits – partly through euphoria that it was all over, and partly because it was SO bad…well; it had been quite good really.

There was absolutely no chance of me risking another coach tour the next day though, which is why I spent it on ship. This turned out to be a good thing for two reasons. Firstly my visit to the gym happily coincided with that of a Russian cabaret contortionist called Valerie, whose act had held my attention for longer than was decent the previous evening. I shall leave the details of that encounter to your imagination though, because I have less salacious fish to fry. You see, by staying onboard I also learned about the ships funnel, and how you can use it to make a great deal of money.

Let me explain.

When we got back from dinner that evening, amongst the events announced in the newsletter for the following day was a free 45 minute seminar on the subject of boosting metabolism, hosted by the ships fitness instructors. Now that's something that interests me – not because I want to lose weight, but because I'm incredibly greedy and would like to eat a lot more and stay the same. So my wife and I decided to go along. I refuse to reveal her motivation for going, on the grounds that doing so could result in me having to recover my testicles from a place God never intended them to be located.

Anyway, the seminar provided some very useful information, but I figured out its true purpose within about 3 minutes of the start. I'm not sure whether anyone else did. My wife certainly didn't.

The instructor talked about exercise and nutrition, but made clear that in his opinion, none of this could be effective if the body was in a toxic state. He then proceeded to tell us about all the aspects of modern life which would create this toxicity. We had no way of knowing how toxic our bodies were, but guess what? He had a simple test we could take. All we needed to do was make an appointment with him, (He'd already collected our names and cabin numbers at the start of the session) and for £45, all would be revealed. Because good health is a family issue, couples could take the test on a two for one deal.

I'd estimate that around 40% of the people attending signed up for the test, including my wife. I didn't go myself. You see I already knew the result – and what was coming next.

Sure enough, she returned from the test the next day, declaring that her body was indeed in a toxic state, and clutching a pile of products which would rectify the situation. I won't tell you what they cost – it's too early…the pain is still too raw…but it was a lot more than the cost of the diagnostic test.

I'm not sure whether it's obvious what happened here – or how it can be used or adapted – so I'll spell out the process. It's an excellent example of a marketing funnel in operation.

The first stage in any marketing funnel is to attract a large number of prospects in at the top of the funnel. The easiest way to do this is to offer them a valuable product or service for free. The ships fitness instructors offered a free seminar on increasing metabolism, and in so doing, ensured that they had a room full of people who would be good prospects for what they ultimately hoped to sell.

An important consideration here is that the product/ service/seminar has to deliver on its promise. It must have value, independent of the sales pitch which it will inevitably precede. If people feel cheated, they will not be open to what's on offer. In this case, the seminar provided some valuable and useful information about metabolism.

The second stage is to offer a reasonably low priced product, related to the original free product/service or seminar. In this case, it was the toxicity test. The seminar raised the question in people's minds…"Is my body toxic, and could it be stopping me from losing weight?" The fitness instructors were on hand to provide answers.

The third stage of the funnel is then to sell higher value products to the people who progressed to level two. In this instance, it was a range of nutritional supplements.

Why is this called a funnel? Because that's an excellent image to convey what's happening. A large number of people are poured in at the top (the free seminar) as the funnel narrows, a smaller number progress through to stage two (the toxicity test) and then as the funnel narrows further, a smaller number still go on to spend more money (the nutritional supplements).

Now with this particular funnel, we're only looking at three stages, but the reality is that a funnel can have any number of stages. The next stage could be an enhanced nutritional system at a higher price. The stage after that could be a fully monitored mentoring programme for £1,000 a year. I have no idea whether they have additional funnel stages in place…but the fitness instructors now have contact details for all their new customers so it would be foolish if there aren't.

The beauty of a funnel marketing system is that it maximises the revenue from each prospective customer, while fully satisfying the individual information and product needs of everyone in the funnel.

From a marketing perspective, it's also a very predictable system. Once you've gone through the process a couple of times, you can predict fairly accurately what the overall revenue and profit will be for each person coming in at the top of the funnel. From there, it's very easy to work out how much it's worth investing to attract someone into the funnel in the first place.

In an increasingly crowded market place, creating a predictable funnel system which simultaneously builds goodwill and customer satisfaction, while maximising the revenue and profit from each individual customer, could give you an all-important edge.

I'll leave you to consider how this might fit in to your own business model - and to marvel at the pain and misery I'm prepared to endure just to bring these marketing insights to you. If it hadn't been for the five star accommodation, Michelin standard food, and wall to wall sunshine, I really don't think I'd have survived at all.

Confessions Of A Semi-Formal Tramp

If you catch me on a day where I'm being totally candid, I'll grudgingly admit to falling just a tad short of total perfection. And one of the areas in which it could be argued that there's a little room for improvement, is in my attention to matters sartorial.

Now I'm sure, like me, you've heard people say they have clothes that are older than their children – and that may be true. But I doubt that those children have now left home and university and are several years into their careers. I have a jacket I bought in 1984. I still wear it.

The above may go some way to explain my wife's concern when she received the itinerary for the cruise we just got back from. It was my first cruise, we booked quite late, and the itinerary didn't arrive until a few days before we were due to depart.

"Think you'd better have a look at this," she said, handing me a rather swish, nicely bound document.

The first thing I saw was a section headed 'packing advice'. The first three words were music to my ears…'Keep It Simple', it said. Fantastic! I always keep it simple…shorts, jeans and T shirts and a jumper if it gets cold. One pair of sandals, one pair of trainers and a pair of casual shoes to travel in. That's it.

The next section was a little more worrying though…and completely at odds with the 'Keep It Simple', advice I'd just read. It was headed 'Dress Code', and detailed some pretty specific requirements for dinner each evening.

There would be three separate dress codes in the evenings – formal, semi formal and smart casual. And these would alternate throughout the cruise. In other words, I'd need to pack something for each. A quick perusal of the criteria confirmed the worst - none of the stuff I'd normally pack fitted into any of these categories.

And to make matters worse, I wasn't really sure what it all meant.

I understood formal – a dinner jacket or business suit. It was a little galling to see 'National dresses added to the list though. I'm sure I don't have to tell you that this is the 'get out of jail free card' for anyone who's got a distant Scottish cousin - or has simply visited Dundee. I was tempted to wrap an old car blanket round my waist, throw on a string vest (a la Rab C Nesbitt) and claim some Caledonian roots, but I didn't have the nerve.

The semi-formal was a little harder to fathom – 'tailored trousers, shirt and smart jacket' for gentlemen it said, and 'elegant dresses for ladies. When do trousers become 'tailored'? Are some of them knocked up by architects or welders, I wondered? And who's to judge whether a dress is elegant? I half expected my wife being stopped at the door to the restaurant... "Excuse me madam, that dress is very nice, but it's not really elegant – now is it?"

It was the 'smart casual' option that really left me the most bemused though. I'm quoting here from the itinerary......

"Stylish resort or leisure wear is ideal'.

What the hell is stylish resort or leisure wear? I have no idea. And are they two different things? Is stylish resort wear different from stylish leisure wear, and if so – in what way? It did make clear that replica football shirts were unacceptable, but I already knew that. Replica football shirts are never acceptable, except in Poundland, Cash Converters, and similar venues where ordinary folk gather to drink cheap cider, compare tattoos and swap benefit fiddling tips. I have one myself for this very purpose.

I needed help, and toyed with the idea of going into Top Shop and asking the first multi-pierced assistant..."Excuse me young lady, but would you be so kind as to direct me to the stylish resort and leisure wear section? I'm going on a cruise and looking for something ideal" But I didn't, mainly because I suspect it would have been a fruitless conversation, resulting in me being asked whether I was taking the piss.

Add into the mix, the fact that one of the formal evenings would be a 'black and white evening', and one of the smart casual evenings would be a 'tropical evening', and you'll begin to understand why this was turning into something of a nightmare for someone like me. Keep it simple? They were having a laugh. And did they honestly think that a bloke from Rotherham would own any piece of clothing that could be described as 'tropical'? I did spill a tin of pineapple down my front once, but I don't think that really counts. And the shirt's been washed now anyway.

So I packed what I'd got and hoped for the best.

Now I've been in hotels and restaurants before where there's supposed to be a dress code, and hardly anyone bothers sticking to it. I expected this to be the same, but it wasn't. Everyone had obviously taken careful note of what they were supposed to wear and when they were supposed to wear it. And I found this very interesting.

You see, we were all allocated a dining table at the start of the cruise, and so you got to see the same people sitting in the same place for dinner. The only difference was that each evening they were adhering to a different dress code. And yet to the casual observer, it was a completely different room of people – such was the dramatic difference that the change of clothes had made. Not just different people, but a different type of people with differing perceptions gained with regard to their income, wealth, lifestyle and social standing.

To someone like me, who rarely pays any attention to such matters, this was something of a revelation. Of course we're all aware of the difference it makes when someone we know 'scrubs up', but the impact is softened by what we already know about them. They can't really fool us. But to experience a group of strangers undergoing such rapid transformations, brings home the perception shift which changing the mode of dress can have.

Mark Twain said that 'Clothes makketh the man.' I'm not sure what he was talking about when he said it, but there can be little doubt that they are a key factor in first impressions, and the way that you are perceived by others – at least in the short term.

If you're in a field where you need to make excellent first impressions, what you wear could be the simplest and easiest way to get off on the right foot. When your business or career depends upon it, it's just not good enough to take the view that it doesn't really matter...that it's what you can do that counts...that people will have to take you as you are. If you do that, you might just as well hand money over to your competitors on a plate.

Now that doesn't mean that 'suited and booted' is the way to go. The ultimate dress code for you will depend on the business you're in and the impression you need to create. But there's little doubt that neglecting this key area can put you at an immediate disadvantage. With so many potential pitfalls on the road to securing customers and business, it would be a shame to fall at such an easily avoidable hurdle.

On that note, I think I'd better get my self down to Primark with my credit card – before it's too late!

15 Minutes Of Fame

Until two weeks ago, there wasn't a single ex pupil of my old school who would get recognised outside his own living room. It was a complete fame-free zone. No singers, no actors, no sports stars, no TV presenters...not even so much as a Big Brother contestant...

And then a fortnight ago, one 'old boy' became -very briefly - just about the most recognised and talked about person in the country. His face adorned just about every front page. Everyone seemed to have an opinion about what he'd done, and in his absence, the press besieged his family and friends looking for insights into his character and motivation.

No...no...it wasn't Raoul Moat. What kind of school do you think I went to? The man in question is Howard Webb, the bloke who took charge of an event in which about a dozen Dutchmen seemingly got lost on the way to a martial arts contest, and found themselves in the middle of a football match.

Before the World Cup final, only hard core football fans knew who Howard Webb was. Two days later, even your granny knew who he was, and what he looked like.

I'll come back to Howard Webb in a moment, but first, I want to tell you about something else...

A couple of years ago, I was involved in arranging the premiere of a film in the west end. I knew nothing about the mechanics of this at all, having only ever seen these events on TV, with glamorous stars walking up the red carpet and flash guns popping. What I didn't know is that many of the people 'invited' to attend are actually paid to be there – and they're often paid quite a lot. Not only that, but some of them don't even bother to see the film. They get dressed in their finery, smile for the cameras, walk in through the front doors - and then out through the back into a waiting taxi. The value of their work is measured in the column inches their attendance secures in the following days newspapers.

Now who would you imagine you'd REALLY want to walk up your red carpet...Tom Cruise, Meryl Streep or someone like that perhaps? That's what I thought. Well believe it or not, the number one targets at the time we were doing this ...the people guaranteed to get the crowds flocking and those all important column inches, were the X Factor finalists and some empty headed bimbo who had just been kicked out of the Big Brother house.

Why?

Because they were flavour of the month...or to be more accurate, flavour of the week. And this newness or novelty value, combined with the massive national exposure they'd had, temporarily made them a very valuable commodity.

Now, fast forward a couple of years, and those same X Factor finalists and Big Brother contestants have probably returned to the obscurity from whence they came. But for a very brief period, they were presented with a window of opportunity. It was a window they could either climb through, to a different life on the other side, or stare blankly at, and wait for someone to slam it shut. To take the former option they would need to move fast. They'd need to gain a foothold, in what would otherwise be, a temporary elevated position.

Howard Webb has been presented with a similar opportunity – the opportunity to transcend the world of refereeing, and to become a 'personality'. Will he take it...does he want it even? I have no idea, but the opportunity is undoubtedly there for him. To take advantage of it, he needs to start taking action now – while his star is still high in the sky. The harsh and fast moving nature of these things means that his star was already on the wane 3 days after the final, and it's falling by the day. He needs to get a foothold as soon as possible.

So what's all this got to do with you?

Andy Warhol said that "In the future, everyone will be world-famous for 15 minutes." I'm not sure what he was talking about when he said it, but the future is here. There's little doubt that the proliferation of media, and the internet in particular, means that there are more opportunities to become 'famous' than ever before - and also that this fame is likely to be short-lived.

Upload a video to Youtube, and if it catches on, it could be seen by millions of people around the world. Other mainstream media could pick it up, and within 48 hours, your name and face could be on the radar of a vast proportion of the developed world. But do nothing more, and it will all be forgotten just as quickly, as someone else moves in to enjoy their own 15 minutes.

Here's the trick you need to play though – use your new found lofty position as a stepping stone to something more enduring. Otherwise you'll end up on your backside, back where you started.

At some point in your life, business or career, you'll probably find yourself thrust into uncharted territory - a prominence to which you're unaccustomed. It may not be the prominence of a World Cup Final or a prime time TV show, but in your own world it will be just as significant. How you act and react could shape the rest of your life – and you'll have very little time to decide what to do before the window of opportunity slams firmly shut again.

Will you be ready for your own 15 minutes? Or will you act like a rabbit trapped in the car headlights - frozen by fear and only released from your inertia once the critical opportunity-laden moment has passed?

The key to making the most of any opportunity is preparation, and a little forethought here will help ensure that you react in the right way when your 15 minutes arrive.

The Car Boot Sale

A few weeks ago, I visited an antique centre with my wife and daughter. We found a couple of pieces we liked, and I said I'd speak to the owner to see how much I could get them for.

"What do you mean?" said my 11 year old with more than a little alarm in her voice.

I explained that I was going to see how much money I could get knocked off the ticket price.

"You're going to ask for money off?" she said incredulously, "You can't do that, it's SO embarrassing! And it's not like you haven't got enough money to pay for it."

She skulked off into a corner, while I went to talk to the owner and agreed a discount of £50 on the two items…about 15% of the purchase price.

When we got in the car, she was still mortified by the experience. We had words. I explained that there was a very good reason I could afford to pay full price …because I'm not an idiot (she couldn't get to grips with that at all) and don't throw money away. I had a bit of a rant about supply and demand and the ethics and protocol of buying, selling and negotiation. I didn't think my message was getting through very well and decided that a little 'hands on' experience might help to clarify things a bit.

"We'll do a car boot sale," I said "You'll get a better feel for it then."

She wasn't terribly keen at first, but as luck would have it, the new series of Junior Apprentice started a couple of days later. Maybe this entrepreneurship lark wasn't just for old folk after all! The idea took on a whole new allure, and we set the wheels in motion.

Now let me say first of all that I've never sold at a car boot sale before. In fact I've only been to a couple…which was more than enough to realise that most sellers are only there because it's closer than the council tip. The range of tat on offer has to be seen to be believed.

No matter. This was to be an educational trip, and so I rung around a couple of local sites.

"What time do you start?" I asked to the first.

"We open from 4.30." said the lady on the other end

"That's a bit late", I said

"Well it doesn't get light much earlier than that." came the reply.

She meant 4.30am in the morning! Sunday morning!!

There are a few things that might coax me out of bed on a Sunday morning at 4 o clock, but the opportunity to flog my rubbish to insomniac strangers for pennies is not one of them. I found another site which opened at a more reasonable 7.00am, and decided to go there instead.

Over a period of a couple of days, we cobbled together quite an impressive collection of 'refuse-in-waiting' which was cluttering up various corners of the house and garage – books, CD's, Toys, pottery, pictures, ornaments…you know the sort of thing. Rather handily, I also had 3 perfectly serviceable suitcases which were now surplus to requirements, following my wife's most recent capitulation in the face of her serious luggage buying fetish. These would be excellent receptacles, to carry everything else, I decided. There was a flaw in this plan, which was only to come to light later.

Anyway, I crammed everything in to the car, set the alarm for 6.15am, and come Sunday morning we set off for the sale site a few miles away, aiming to get there for 7.00am. The roads were deserted and I half expected arriving to see a bloke in a luminous jacket standing in an empty field. But as we turned a corner, a whole new hidden world emerged. It was like everyone who wasn't asleep had descended on this one spot. Another 5 minutes and we'd have been too late for a pitch.

I paid my £7 entrance fee to the man in the luminous jacket, (he was there – just in a much busier field than I'd imagined) parked up in one of the final two rows, and started unloading our crap...sorry, stock...onto the patio table I'd borrowed for the purpose. Apparently, a wallpaper pasting table is the de rigour piece of equipment for this job, but I don't own one for pretty much the same reason that I don't own a polar bear trap – I'm never going to use it.

As we started to unload the car, about half a dozen hobgoblin type characters emerged from nowhere, trying to find hidden gems ahead of the crowd. This was more than a little annoying, particularly when one of them tried to buy the folding chair we'd brought to sit on! I responded to their requests for prices with..."Fifty quid now, but it might be cheaper when we've GOT THE BLOODY STOCK OUT!" and this seemed to do the trick. Ten minutes later, we had a fully functioning...if very amateurish...car boot stall.

Now there was another flaw in my plan which I haven't told you about yet. I don't really like 'outside' and there was no doubt about it...this car boot sale was in a field. I've never been able to see the point of outside – why people get all excited about it. I mean, if you're sitting in an air conditioned and heated building or car, you're in control. You can have the light and temperature just as you want it. It won't be windy and you won't be bothered by insects. And you've got somewhere comfy to sit or lay down. You have a choice. I like it. But outside – well that's a totally different kettle of fish.

You're at the mercy of the weather for one thing. I've noticed there are all sorts of weather conditions, and here's the point – there's only one very specific combination of factors that make me happy...about 20 degrees centigrade, slightly overcast and with no wind. A bit like inside really. Anything else is just too hot, too cold, too bright, too dark, too wet, too windy, snowy or 'too something'.

That Sunday morning fell into the 'too hot' category...the hottest day of the year and definitely too hot to be standing in shade-free field for 5 hours. I suspect we may have made considerably more money, had I not spent large parts of the morning sheltering under my Land Rover.

It wasn't a complete financial disaster though…

First thing to go was the Guinea Pig cage. I almost didn't bother taking the former home of the recently departed Henry. It was a big bulky thing, and I didn't think it would sell. It shows what I know, because we could have sold it a dozen times. The bloke, who bought it, left it to collect later and plenty of folk wanted to buy it in the meantime, including a 6'5" giant of a man who was practically in tears at having missed it! Emotions clearly run high at these events.

I'd taken my daughter along to experience a bit of haggling and negotiation, and one of the disappointing things early on, was that few people were prepared to give it a try. They asked for the price, we'd tell them, and then they'd walk away. Presumably they were interested in the item at some price, and if you're asking £3 for it…how far apart can you be? One woman snorted indignantly when I had the audacity to ask £1 for a George Michael double album and stormed off! We looked at each other, both thinking the same thing…"How little did she expect to pay?"

I'd tutored my daughter in advance on some useful phrases to use when negotiating and faced with lowball offers (although she point blank refused to say "How much??? You're 'avin me eyes ahht!!!" in a mock cockney accent for some reason) but at this rate, it didn't look like she was going to get to use any of it.

Thank goodness for the eastern Europeans then, who aren't nearly so reticent.

A Kosovan bloke came along and expressed an interest in the suitcases. He called his wife over who was clearly the chief negotiator. Although she spoke virtually no English, she coped very well by simply knowing what half of the price was and then offering that for everything. I tried to defuse this with a bit of humour, but unsurprisingly this got a bit lost in the translation, and was met with "No, I give you £13". We eventually reached agreement at £15, and they went happily on their way – but not before trying to buy a meat cleaver at a third of the price asked, whilst wielding it menacingly in my direction.

As they left with two suitcases, I couldn't help pondering on this...before I'd left home that morning; I'd checked my company online orders for the weekend. They came to just over £20,000. And yet there I was, standing in a roasting hot field at 9.00am on a Sunday morning arguing with a Kosovan over a quid! Perhaps there's a lesson there – often it's not about the money, it's about the winning. If you can find some way of letting the other side win, while getting the money...perhaps everyone wins.

Anyway, we were on a roll now. My daughter was getting involved in the sales process, skilfully splitting the difference with a lady who was trying to knock down the price on a globe, and adjusting the prices she was asking for things in response to the reaction she was getting from browsers. She was starting to realise that prices aren't fixed, and that they depend on good old fashioned supply and demand. Things are worth exactly what people are prepared to pay.

The final suitcase went to a nice Asian lady, and a couple of dozen other items were snapped up for pennies in the pound. For some reason though, the dolls pushchair just wouldn't sell. At least 10 people had come and looked at it, asked the price...a full £8...and then walked away. My daughter was becoming increasingly frustrated by this, but little did I know that when I left her on her own for a few minutes to peruse some of the delights available on some of the other stalls, (slightly used toilet seat anyone?) that she would resort to dirty tactics.

I returned to find her in conversation with a mother and 3 year old. It was clear that the child wanted the push chair, but the mum was reluctant to buy. Eventually, she gave in and the money was handed over.

"Well done" I said after they'd left, "How did you do that?"

"It was easy" she replied "I attracted the attention of the 3 year old while her mums back was turned, showed her the push chair and then let pester power do the rest."

In just 2 weeks, she'd gone from being appalled at me asking for a discount in an antique shop, to blatantly targeting sneaky sales tactics at the under 5's. I didn't know whether to be proud or ashamed!

The crowds thinned, and just when all right-thinking people were emerging from their Sunday morning lay in, it was time to go home. We'd made a grand total of £76.25, but learned lessons that were worth an awful lot more. More about those later.

Just one problem though…

We hadn't sold everything – in fact we hadn't sold half of it. And it had all arrived packed in the suitcases I'd sold to the intransigent Kosovan and her husband. I won't dwell on the implication of having dozens of books, CD's DVD's , toys and other assorted paraphernalia floating loose in the back of a Land Rover as you weave your way home down country roads, but I'm sure you know what they are. Let's just say that a detour via the dump would have been the most sensible option in retrospect.

As our remaining stock clattered from one side of the car to the other, father and daughter discussed what had been learned from the day. Here's what we came up with between us:

1. Products don't have single fixed value.

The price you can sell any product for will depend purely on supply and demand, and the place you choose to sell your product will have a big impact. Items have a lower value at car boot sales than just about anywhere else. We had a very nice handbag for sale (not my colour, but you know what I mean!) which attracted more than a dozen women who asked the price. Each one balked at the £5 quoted, despite the fact that it would have cost over £50 new and would have easily sold for £10+ in a second hand retail environment, or indeed on eBay.

The lesson is that by doing nothing more than moving a product from one market to another, you can sometimes multiply the selling price. The question to ask yourself is whether you offering your products to the most lucrative market? If you're not making as much money as you'd like, a shift in market could make all the difference.

2. Newness is a strong sales motivator.

When we first arrived at the sale, people descended on the car to see what we had. It was all new to the market and they wanted to be first. Successful companies know all about this, which is why they are constantly introducing new products and updated versions of existing products (often which are practically the same as the original.)

Is there some way you can use the power of 'new' in your business? It might mean creating a new product, a new version of your existing product, new packaging or even simply introducing your old product to a group of people to whom it is new. Newness gives sales a boost in myriad ways and it's well worthwhile giving thought to how you can introduce newness into your enterprise as often as possible.

3. The threat of losing an opportunity is a strong sales motivator

The busiest time on the stall (apart from when we arrived) was when we started to pack up to leave. People saw the opportunity to buy being snatched away from them and this piqued their interest. Once again, this isn't confined to car boot stalls. Its human nature to want what you can't have and you can't have something if it's being taken away.

A central tenet of many marketing strategies is to emphasise scarcity...this offer is about to be withdrawn, we only have 10 of these left, once these are sold there will be no more at the price, this offer is open for the next few hours only...and they work because of this human trait. People want what they can't have, or which they risk losing for ever.

Is this something you could incorporate in your business? Paradoxically, by withdrawing something from sale and telling people about it, you might actually sell more.

4. You need to remove barriers

If you stand in front of your stock with your arms folded, people are reluctant to approach. You need to make browsing as unthreatening as possible, and the way to do that is to stand well back, or better still, off to the side. They can then be approached for a sale once they feel safe and comfortable. I think there's a metaphor here for just about every business. You must allow your potential customers 'space' to assess and evaluate what you're offering in an un-pressured and non-threatening environment. So are you doing that? Or do you go straight for the jugular at the first sniff of interest? And if you do, are you driving people away?

5. People will instinctively follow the crowd

When the stall was busy, even more people flocked around. Getting the first person to come was far more difficult though. My daughter cottoned on to this very quickly and decided to start acting like a customer, browsing through the stock. It worked a treat. The public see one person looking and think, "Maybe there's something of interest here! I'll take a look too." There's a 'safety in numbers' element to this behaviour too, I think.

Could this be useful to you? Of course it could. You don't need to have a physical business with flesh and blood customers standing in front of you to take advantage of this. For example, the use of testimonials in mail order serves exactly the same purpose – "If other people are interested, maybe there's something here for me too." If you don't have a 'crowd' yet, it's worth giving some thought to how you might attract one. Even if your initial crowd are spending little or no money, they will attract the attention of those that will.

It had been an interesting and educational morning, if tiring and not particularly lucrative. As we pulled up wearily on the drive, my wife met us at the car and peered inside. "Hmm, you've got quite a lot left," she said, "Never mind, it will do for next time."

I didn't know whether to laugh, cry or set about her with the unsold meat cleaver!

Viking's Revenge

Some time around the mid 1980's, three middle aged blokes called Bjorn, Olaf, and Sven were sitting in an office on an industrial estate in southern Sweden. It was winter and it was Scandinavia, so it was dark and cold and miserable. The three men were bored, depressed, and as appears to be the predisposition of a lot of their countrymen, considering ending it all.

As the snow continued to pile up outside, their conversation turned to the decline of their country in the world order over the past millennium. Just 1,000 years or so ago, their Viking ancestors were a force to be reckoned with - striking fear into the hearts of men women and children throughout Europe as they raided, raped and pillaged their way through the continent. Everywhere they went, they left misery and despair in their wake. If only they could return to those days and make an impact. That would cheer them up.

But times have changed. Lands that they previously colonised, developed and became more powerful. You can't just turn back the clock. It's hard to start throwing your weight around when your potential conquest has nuclear weapons, and all you have, is some pickled Herring.

The three of them slumped in their chairs, staring into space for what seemed like hours, and then all of a sudden, Olaf sat bolt upright. "I have it!" he said, his voice quivering with excitement "There is more than one way to skin a Reindeer." "I know…" said Sven who was just about to reveal the three ways he had used personally (one involving a Stanley knife, a piece of thick rope and a winch) when Olaf stopped him short. "No, no, no, I mean we do not necessarily need to go raiding, pillaging, colonising and all that malarkey to strike fear into the hearts of men and women throughout Europe…to leave pain, misery and distress in our wake. There is an easier way…a modern way."

I don't have any cast iron proof of any of this, but I'm convinced that it almost certainly happened. How else do you explain that just a short while later in early 1987, the first Ikea store was opened in Britain, and many more were to follow? There can be no other explanation for their existence. If you were seeking to create the most soul destroying, energy sapping and spirit defeating experience...but one which people would actually enter into voluntarily...you could do no finer job.

On that snowy day back in the mid 1980's, Bjorn Olaf and Sven created something extraordinary, and last Saturday I was cursing them for it. Because for reasons I won't bore you with here, I found myself in the passenger seat of a battered long wheel base Transit van, in some god forsaken corner of the west midlands with £2,000 in my pocket and a very long shopping list. Ikea loomed into view.

I know what you're thinking. Why is someone supposedly worth a bob or two, roughing it in a starship-miled Transit and about to enter hell on purpose? Well all I can say is that I'm obviously much nicer than you may have been led to believe, and have a heart of gold. That's my story and I'm sticking to it.

I don't know whether you've shopped at Ikea but let me give you some idea of what to expect if you haven't - and torture you mentally by returning you to the scene of past torments if you have.

The first thing you need to know – and this is important – is that as soon as you've committed yourself to going through the doors, you're not going to get out of there any time soon. If it's not busy you might get out within an hour. If it is busy, well cancel your plans for the day. You see the whole thing is designed like a giant one way maze. Once you're in, there's no way back and no obvious shortcut to the end. I should add here that there ARE secret doors which can cut several miles from your journey, but no sane person would visit the store often enough to discover where they are. So shop with a lunatic if you want to get out fast.

But I digress. If you're a normal person, as soon as you're through the door, you're committed to a very long walk if you want to get out again. And believe me, you will. You'll be desperate to get out.

At the start of your journey you will be encouraged to pick up a short sturdy pencil and what looks for the entire world like a betting slip. This is a shopping list you're expected to fill out as you travel around the store, marking down the wonderful things you've seen and would like to buy. Except you can't. What you can buy though, is a box of bits and an Allen key. And be very clear about this…every item you mark down on that list has the potential to send your blood pressure through the roof, and take you to the very edge of your mental endurance.

Now, there's something pre-printed on that shopping list I haven't told you about yet. You might not notice it at first. It's a couple of innocuous looking boxes labelled 'aisle' and 'location'. I'll return to these later. What they represent has reduced grown men to tears. But we haven't even got to that part yet. Because all we've done so far is to get into the store, pick up an order form and start marking down our 'wish list'.

When you've shopped in Ikea for any length of time, you start to appreciate how sheep and cattle must feel when they are herded down fenced off channels at market. The walkways are very narrow, with only the occasional opportunity to breathe as it opens into a 'clearing'. The clearing is usually littered with dining tables or sofas, but it's a welcome release. Like an oasis in the dessert – albeit one polluted by piles of camel dung.

About half way around a REAL oasis appears – the restaurant! Now up until this point, you will have seen no natural light since you walked through the doors. There are no windows. But the restaurant gives you a tantalising glimpse - just when you may have been on the brink of giving up hope - of a world outside Ikea.

There are windows in the restaurant - with glass in them. Okay, the view may be of the car park, but you can see real people who have escaped. If they can do it so can you. When Olaf hatched his plan back in Sweden, this is exactly what he wanted you to think. He didn't want to break you - not yet while he had more pain to impart.

Hardly anyone walks past the restaurant, any more than they would if it were a real oasis in a real desert. And for the same reasons. You're not really sure when or if you'll get an opportunity to take on food and water again. The end is nowhere in sight and you have no idea how long it might take you to get there. It would be madness to pass up the opportunity to take on fuel. Seasoned campaigners also know they have yet to face the warehouse ordeal

– more of which later – and so partly to gather their strength, and partly to delay the inevitable, they sit in hunched groups around tables wearing the haunted look of condemned men.

When we staggered into the restaurant last Saturday, weak, and hungry and thirsty, I half expected to be handed some cooking utensils, some raw ingredients and a camping stove…but no, the hot food was pre-cooked, the sandwiches pre-packed and the drinks already made. Even Ikea haven't come up with the idea of you making your own food yet, but I suspect it may only be a matter of time.

Five minutes later we were back on the trail, the temptations to put off the inevitable overcome by the desire to just get it over with. The rest of the wish list was filled out over the next hour as we fought our way through department after department offering just about everything you could possibly think of, and quite a lot that you'd rather not. After what seemed like an eternity, we could see the end of the showrooms coming tantalisingly into view.

Now to the first time visitor, this must give the same sense of euphoria experienced by marathon runners as they catch sight of the finishing line for the first time. But it's a euphoria which is short lived. Imagine if you'd just run 26 miles and could see the finish line in front of you, and then someone tapped you on the shoulder and said "Sorry mate, you're only half way. Oh, and you've got to do the last bit with a sack of coal on your back."

That's what it feels like when you hit the warehouse!

The purpose of those 'aisle' and 'location' numbers you've been painstakingly writing down for the last two hours becomes clear – you've now got to go in to a cavernous warehouse, find the things you want to buy, and load them on to a trolley yourself. Now that's inconvenient (but not impossible) if you're buying a few bits and pieces, but what if you're buying a three seater sofa, armchair, king sized bed, dining table and chairs, coffee table, bed side cabinets and book case? What if you're buying all of that and a lot more besides? The same rules apply. You're on your own pal.

I won't document what happened over the next half hour as we sweated and strained to bundle a full transit van load of merchandise from the warehouse shelves on to 3 huge trolleys and then steer them through the warehouse to the checkout, but suffice to say it involved a fair amount of bad temper, bad language and written- in-blood oaths never to darken this stores doorstep with our presence again. How you manage if you're old, disabled have a bad back or are just a bit of a wimp, I have no idea.

Anyway, we wrestled everything on to the trolleys and through the checkouts where we were handed another piece of paper to take to a collection point. Even Ikea have realised that you can't expect members of the public to hoist 3 seater sofas from warehouse shelves onto trolleys on their own. I was given a number at the help desk, and another 10 minute wait followed, during which I occupied myself by marvelling at how much confidence the 20 stone woman opposite must have to be eating such a massive hotdog in public without a hint of embarrassment.

My number was called and three more huge trolleys were wheeled out containing the sofa and other assorted paraphernalia which for some unknown reason were considered unsuitable to be picked up from the warehouse. I looked at it and sighed…"Do you have many people committing suicide in here?" I asked the woman behind the counter. "They come close…" she said "…they come close.

Wheeling the first trolley out of the doors in to the cold but fresh air felt (I'd imagine) like being let out of prison. We quickly loaded up the van and drove the half hour back to Sutton Coldfield. Once it was unloaded at the other end, pretty much without incident, (apart from the inevitable pantomime that always precedes threading an 8 foot sofa through a 6'6" door with no room for manoeuvre) we set about unpacking what we'd bought. The armchair was first. What could go wrong with that? We were about to find out.

The first two covers went on easily, but the third was obviously the wrong shape. I rang the store. Could they send a replacement? Of course they couldn't. The only option available was to go back. Never mind, just a quick 5 minute trip to customer services. That's what you'd think.

When I arrived at customer services, it was 4.00pm and the guy behind the desk had clearly had a hard day. He had the look and manner of someone who might snap at any moment and bludgeon a customer to death with a faulty chair leg. "All I can do for you," he said when I explained my problem "is give you your money back. You'll have to go back into the store to ask advice on what you need."

Back into the store!

I could have cried at this point, but wouldn't give them the satisfaction. So I trooped back into the theatre of nightmares, found an assistant who gave me a nice print out of what I needed to take to the checkout. They would then give me another piece of paper to take back to customers services (yes, really!) where I could pick up my new cover.

Unfortunately, my journey back to the checkout wasn't without hindrance. The customers in the morning (with the exception of Hotdog Woman) had been a pretty athletic bunch....steely eyed, lithe Ikea veterans launching SAS style smash and grab raids. Moving fast and focussed on the task in hand... But now it was late afternoon and the Birmingham chapter of the Cream Cake and Lard Appreciation Society had dragged its collective carcass from its pit, and was blocking my path at every turn.

I wanted to get to the checkout fast, and considered two options, both taken from the world of sport – I could try to force my way through like an American football running back, or set off on a jinking run a la welsh rugby wizard Barry John circa 1972. Having spent a lot of money on my teeth, a chose the latter and was back at the checkout within 15 minutes – a personal best. They gave me the bit of paper promised by the girl back up on the shopfloor, and there I was back where I started – waiting to see the harassed bloke on customer service.

Now if you have shopped at Ikea, one thing you will have noticed is the weird and wonderful Scandinavian sounding names they give to their products...Duktig dining tables, Galej glasses, Kivsta cushions - that kind of thing. A red face, squat bloke in front of me in the queue appeared to be having problems with a Fooken chair and a Bastod coffee table he'd bought the previous week. That's what is sounded like anyway, but I couldn't be sure. It wasn't that easy to tell because of the froth coming out of his mouth. He wasn't happy with them though; I could tell that much.

Eventually it was my turn, and I wearily handed over my piece of paper to the same fella who said he couldn't help me before. An assistant was despatched into the shop and came back with the same thing I'd brought back – but this time it was dirty into the bargain. Mr Harassed said he was perplexed and said he would get someone from the shopfloor to come and sort it out. Five minutes later, the same assistant who I'd seen half an hour earlier (she obviously knew a shortcut she'd neglected to tell me about) emerged and found out what I needed. The only problem was that they only had one left, and that had a small stain on it as well.

Normally I wouldn't have put up with this, but they'd battered, beaten and bewildered me now. The plan hatched by Bjorn, Sven and Olaf back in that office in the mid 1980's had fully come to fruition. Victory was theirs, and they hadn't even had to break sweat. I walked out into the rain clutching my slightly stained cushion covers, pathetically grateful to have at least got something for my trouble.

Am I the only person to suffer like this? I think not. And yet despite providing what I am pretty confident is just about the worst shopping experience imaginable, Ikea is phenomenally successful - not just in the UK, but around the world.

Why is that? Well the key reasons, may provide a clue to a potential breakthrough for any small business or enterprise

There's little doubt that despite everything I've said here, Ikea products are by and large, pretty good quality, and excellent value for money. How is that achieved? Well in part by providing the lousy customer experience I just described! An Ikea customer has to do an awful lot for himself - choose the products, find them in a warehouse, load them on to a trolley, carry them to the car or van…and then turn them from a bag of bits into something you can sit on, sleep on, eat off or look at when he gets home. If he has a problem…he has a problem. Customer service isn't great.

But in return for all this misery, the customer gets a well designed and reasonably manufactured product at an excellent price. And that is evidently an acceptable trade off for a large proportion of the population - most specifically, those on a budget.

Is this a piece of information and insight you could use in your business? Are there frills your customers would willingly give up in return for a discount? Might your customers be prepared to buy an 'unfinished' product or service if they could get it a lot cheaper? Is there a gap in your particular market for someone to come in and undercut everyone by asking customers to do a bit more for themselves?

I'll leave you to ponder on that as we come to the second big reason why Ikea is so popular. You can have it today! People are impatient. When they see something, they don't want it next week or next month. They don't want to wait for some lazy artisan in France or Italy to, amble back from a long lunch of wine and cheese before chipping away at a piece of wood for weeks on end. They're shopping because they want it now, and Ikea gives them the opportunity to get it.

So what about the business that you're in? Are customers sometimes keen to get hold of the product or service quicker than it's usually supplied? Is there some way you can let them have it today...and if not today, much quicker than it's usually turned around? And if you could do that, do you think you might attract a lot more business, simply because you can supply it NOW?

These two factors of immediate delivery and frill-free value arc central to Ikea's success. It's impossible for me to speculate on what they might mean to your specific business, but I'd wager they mean something to most. And in your case, it could be something which gives you the unique selling proposition you've been looking for, and turns your enterprise from an also ran to a market leader.

If it happens, please let me know. I really need to start healing some of the mental scar inflicted by Olaf and his mates. I need to know I didn't suffer last Saturday without purpose.

The Real Joy Of Christmas

There are some words in the English language that have a visceral effect. They don't just enter through the ears and get processed by the brain. They have a much deeper physical impact - one which can be felt in the pit of the stomach. I'm sure you've experienced this yourself. On Saturday, my wife hit me with two of those words and then really kicked me in the guts by preceding them with "Let's go to a..." Talk about hitting where it hurts...

The two words were 'Christmas' and 'market'.

I could write a book, devoted to nothing more than what is wrong with Christmas, but suffice to say that when December 27th arrives, it's met with the sort of feeling I'd imagine you get after being released by Islamic extremist kidnappers. And as for markets, well, my appetite for cheap tat was fully satisfied around about 1978, and I don't expect to get hungry again any time soon. So putting the two things together...cheap tat and Christmas...and then bringing it together in one place is truly terrifying, especially if you're expected to go there.

I explored all the usual escape routes. The weather can often be relied upon to scupper a trip like this in December, but the sky was annoyingly clear and blue. In desperation I went online looking for an accident blocking the motorway (that always happens to me when I'm on the way to somewhere I actually want to go) but for once, everyone had been driving like the day they passed their test. I briefly flirted with the old standby of feigning illness, but decided against it. Feigned illness can become real injury if you're found out. Experience has taught me that.

And so armed with a fat wallet and a stiff upper lip, we set off to explore the delights of the Lincoln Christmas market.

Perhaps I should have got a hint of what to expect when, on the outskirts of the city, I was greeted with signs informing me that under no circumstances should I head for the market area and try to park my car. There was no parking to be had. Instead I was directed towards something I have never visited before – and with good reason – a park and ride.

Now I'm sorry, but why would anyone want to do that...park and ride? Why would I want to drive to somewhere I don't want to go, leave my nice warm, comfy car, and get on a cold grotty bus to take me to the place I actually wanted to go in the first place? About 30 years ago, I bought my first car specifically because it was better in every possible way, than a bus. What I like to do is completely the opposite of park and ride...ride (in my car) and park. The whole point of having a car is that it takes you exactly where you want to go, for which you pay a substantial premium over a bus.

Anyway, there was no alternative, and so I followed the signs directing me 4 miles out of town to a muddy field where some bandit parted me with £12 for the privilege of parking in a bog and wading to shore. There then followed a tedious half mile walk through a quagmire, before being herded on to the aforementioned bus back into the town I'd just left in my nice warm comfy car. Lovely.

What's quite funny as I look back now, is that I sat there on that bus thinking "Well things can't get any worse than this." Little did I know that I was experiencing the highlight of the day. Things were about to turn very ugly – in more ways than one.

As we got off the bus...wife and daughter remaining annoyingly optimistic about what was to follow...it became clear that there were a lot of people there. And I mean a LOT. Now I don't know whether you've ever been into Lincolnshire, but there's no avoiding the fact that there are some very strange looking folk about. I've noticed this before. It's probably best that I don't speculate too closely on the reason, other than to say that some of the outlying small villages must have been quite remote in the past, and a lot of young bucks probably weren't very keen on leaving the house for their evening entertainment.

That may explain why on alighting the bus (I don't think you're allowed to just get off) and spotting a public toilet, I found myself in a queue sandwiched between a seven foot giant with hands like wicket keepers gloves, and a hunchback midget. I looked around for the Billy Smarts posters, but there were none to be seen. There were some normal looking people in the queue as well, but I suspect they'd come from over the border from Yorkshire.

Now as a bloke, I'm not used to queuing for a toilet, but as I stood there, inching forward and trying not to annoy the giant by head butting him in the groin, I had cause to wonder why women put up with it. I mean, in my experience, they don't put up with much else these days. Maybe they've just been brainwashed into thinking it's the natural order of things…I am a woman and therefore I shall be forever expected to spend large parts of my life waiting to urinate. Men wouldn't put up with it, that's for sure. If this was a regular occurrence, they'd just do it in the street. We'd soon get bigger toilets then.

Maybe that's what women need to do – a bit of direct action. Come to think of it, quite a few have already started in Rotherham town centre on a Saturday night. But it's a practice that hasn't reached the Lincoln Christmas market yet.

I reached the front of the queue and decided to avoid standing next to the giant, figuring that the experience could be humiliating and dampening in equal measure. I needn't have worried, because he disappeared into a cubicle - an act which I have to say, freshened my enthusiasm for getting out of there fast.

After taking my turn at the stinking trough that passes for a urinal in these places, I went to wash my hands, pausing briefly to look at the hand drying facilities which comprised a soggy, stained towel on a continuous roll. I thought better off it, and escaped out of the door, just as the giant was benefiting from the end result of some devastatingly effective digestive transit. The blokes still stuck in the queue had the look of condemned men.

My wife and daughter were sympathetic when I caught up with them. "Ha, now you know what it's like for us!" they said in unison. As we headed towards the main market area through a street lined with fast food stalls one after the other, my sense of foreboding grew stronger. I looked at the map the bandit had handed to me in exchange for my £12 at the park and ride. We were in what might most accurately be called a rat run. There was no turning back, no turning off, no escaping!

We rounded a corner to be confronted by the sort of heaving crowd I haven't seen since the days before football clubs decided that on balance, it would be better if they had some safety measures in place to avoid crushing their customers to death. Naively, I thought this was just a small bottleneck. It wasn't. As we turned the next corner, the crowds progress slowed to a snails pace, and then to a dead stop.

There was nowhere to go – stalls to the left and right and a huge tide of people both forward and behind. Nobody could move either forwards, backwards or sideways. We were trapped and a few people were starting to panic. For a moment, I feared for our safety. It would have only taken some pushing from behind and people could very easily have been trampled. It happens. But eventually, bit by bit, the crowd started to move again, and as we edged forward, I think everyone was united by one thought. They just wanted to get out.

After what seemed like an age, we reached something approaching a clearing....by that I mean that you could now inhale without physically touching someone else...but even my wife and daughters appetite for shopping had gone now. We commenced the slow crawl towards the end of the market and back to the bus. We hadn't even seen anything (unless you count a giant and a hunchback midget) let alone bought anything.

As we got back to the bus, thousands more people were pouring in, and it was the same story back at the park and ride mud-fest (as it had now become). I wanted to tell them to turn round and escape while they could, but they probably wouldn't have believed me. And besides, most of them had probably been before, experienced the same hell last year, and still come again.

Why? Because it's a 'Christmas' market. That may be one of my knot-in-the-stomach' words, but to a sizeable percentage of the population it has an irresistible allure. It's an allure that causes them to cast aside their usual common sense and rationality, loosen their purse strings and spend their hard earned money on products, services and events that they wouldn't even consider, at other times of the year.

And why should this be of interest to you and me? Because once we take our 'customer' hat off for a moment and give it some thought, it presents a unique recurring annual opportunity to make a great deal of money that it would be foolish to ignore.

But how do you do it?

Well, much will depend on what business you're already in (if any) and what opportunities that throws up. But here are a few ideas to think about....

1. Create a gift

I think everyone should explore the possibility of creating an adaptation of their product or service, and promote it exclusively as a Christmas gift. This could take the form of a Christmas version of the product, a specially created gift package of the product, or in the case of a service. – A gift voucher for recipients to use a pre-determined amount of the service.

The Christmas gift market is huge, and there's an almost insatiable appetite (mainly created by desperation!) for new gift ideas. It may be that you haven't thought of the output of your business in these terms, but a little lateral thinking could pay massive dividends here.

2. Organise an event

Perhaps you could organise an event linked to your product with a Christmas theme. Often that can involve little more than inserting the word 'Christmas' as a prefix to your event. A 'Computer Fair' for example, takes on a whole new perspective when it becomes a Christmas Computer Fair, because it alerts attendees to the gift potential of what's on offer and reminds them that they have gift buying problems which they need to solve quickly.

3. Launch a temporary venture

It's worth thinking about creating a short term sideline venture in the lead up to Christmas which capitalises on your skills, experience or knowledge. Consumer needs and wants change in the lead up to Christmas. A business importing and selling container loads of remote control toy helicopters may struggle badly as a year round venture, but could be a serious money maker if operated on a fast in-fast out basis on the lead up to Christmas. There are many other products and services which achieve the major part of their sales over a very short pre-Christmas period. There may be one or more of those within your area of expertise and influence.

4. Tweak your marketing.

The pre-Christmas period is a time to make your marketing Crimbo-Friendly. That means drawing full attention to any gift or Christmas celebration related aspects of your products and services – however tenuous. This is a time where a lot on non-Christmas related spending is placed on hold, and so you really need to make the most of what you have by linking it in some way to the festive period.

Hopefully you don't suffer from my aversion to Christmas, and these ideas are just icing on what is a very attractive cake for you. But if you do, perhaps this is the best way to cope…stop seeing yourself as a reluctant customer at Christmas and take steps to become an enthusiastic supplier. I reckon you'd be amazed how much more interesting and tolerable the festive period could become if it was the source of profit rather than pain. And that's what I will be trying to do next year.

I was thinking about none of this when I left that Christmas market though. My mind was filled with the negative aspects of what seemed like a wasted day. But experience has taught me that there are the seeds of something useful in almost every setback. And maybe that's the most important thing to take away from this…a commitment to take a negative experience, reframe it and look at it from a completely different perspective.

There's always another side to the coin, and it can often be very different from the one you've found yourself exposed to.

When Words Don't Matter

I don't usually pay much attention to the lyrics of songs. Blokes don't, do they? It's a woman thing. But as I was driving to work the other day listening to a Ray Charles CD, I half heard some lyrics that really got my attention. I thought I must have misheard, and so rewound to listen again. I hadn't.

The song is from 1949 (Yes I know I need to update my record collection) and called 'Blues before Sunrise. Here's what I heard, which took me by such surprise:

"I love my baby, but she won't behave. I'm going to buy a 45 and send her to her grave."

We hear much today about Gangsta Rappers glorifying guns and violence and we think it's something terrible and new. And yet here's a 60 year old song performed by one of the most respected artists of the 20th century, which suggests that if your girlfriend steps out of line, it's in order to buy a gun and kill her. I may have missed it, but I don't remember anyone getting into a lather about Ray Charles.

Why not? Well, I think there's a very good reason which tells us an awful lot about communication and persuasion. I'll tell you what it is later, but first I want to tell you about something else which is a clue to what I'm talking about.

Last Christmas my Brother in Law bought me a book called Great Speeches. As the title suggests, it's a book which documents, transcribes and discusses the most powerful, famous and influential speeches in history. There's Martin Luther Kings's "I Have a Dream" speech, Churchills "We'll fight them on the beaches speech, Barrack Obama's inauguration speech together with scores of others made by great orators and persuaders like Nelson Mandela, Franklin D Roosevelt, John F Kennedy, Charles De Gaulle and Ghandi.

I was looking forward to reading it. Some of the speeches, I'd seen or heard delivered on film or audio recording, but some of the others, I'd only heard about. But as I read one after the other, the same feeling came over me…

They weren't nearly as impressive as I'd expected them to be…

Much of what was written appeared mundane and uninspiring. In fact the only time I got any sense of the impact the words might have was when I related the words I was reading, to the speech I'd actually seen or heard.

So what's going on here? How did Ray Charles get away with what 50 Cent never could? Why aren't the speeches of King, Churchill and Obama anywhere near as good as they're cracked up to be?

A few weeks ago, I watched a TV programme which provided a massive clue. It was on the subject of autism, something I knew very little about. One of the things people with autism have a problem with, is relating to, and communicating with, other people. And the reason for that is that they find it very difficult to pick up on the nuances of communication which most of us take for granted. Tone of voice, pitch, volume, facial expressions and non verbal gestures don't carry the same meaning for people with autism as they do for the rest of us. And so they don't easily identify the mood of those around them or the real meaning of what they're saying.

Why is this so important?

Because as the programme pointed out, only 10% of the meaning we get from a communication comes from the actual words used. The other 90% comes from the way in which the words are delivered, and other non verbal clues arising out of tone of voice, volume, facial expressions and gestures. Is it any wonder then, that people with autism often have a tough time communicating? They understand the words, but don't understand the meaning.

So if only 10% of the meaning we get from something is derived from the actual words used, it's perhaps no surprise that Ray Charles can express a sentiment in a blues song, and gets a completely different reaction to 50 Cent in a much more aggressively pitched rap. The delivery...and the deliverer...are almost everything.

And similarly, it is perhaps no surprise that all those great speeches, stripped of the vocal skills, pitch, tone, volume, facial expressions and body language of those highly accomplished orators, don't seem so great any more. The delivery...and the deliverer...are almost everything.

All of this can be summed up in a single well worn phrase...

"It's not what you say; it's the way that you say it."

It may be a well worn phrase, but it's no less true for that. The same words delivered in a different way will have dramatically differing impacts on those hearing them.

If your communications...whether they be speeches, sales pitches, presentations, or even regular day to day interactions...are failing to get the desired effect, the chances are that much of the failure is down to the delivery rather than the message itself. And yet the natural reaction is to look to the words when we don't get the reaction we want. The words may be perfectly acceptable, but the delivery is wrong

The obvious lesson here is to look closely at how your key messages are being delivered and received. Is your 'delivery system' doing justice to the words you're using? Or are your words saying one thing, but your delivery, something else?

Killer Tomatoes v Flesh Eating Fly Trap's

On 2nd January 1760, colonial governor Arthur Dobbs was walking through a forest in North Carolina when he discovered something quite extraordinary. It was something that amazed and astounded him, and it has held the same fascination for countless generations over the following 250 years ago.

As Dobbs looked down at his feet he saw a plant, the like of which he had never seen before, and in his diary he wrote the following...

"The greatest wonder of the vegetable kingdom is a curious unknown species. Upon anything touching the leaves, they instantly close like a spring trap. To this surprising plant I have given the name, fly trap."

The Venus fly tap (as it became known) survives in poor soil by enticing flies, moths, beetles and other insects into its jaws, and then violently snapping shut, devouring and digesting its prey. Charles Darwin regarded it as one of the finest examples of evolution in action, and the plant entered and stuck in the public consciousness due to its spectacular modus operandi.

I think most of us are aware of the Venus Fly Trap, and have a perception of what it does, but I'd bet there are few of us that would guess how much it shares in common with the humble tomato plant. You see, hard as it may be to believe, the tomato plant is carnivorous too. It just goes about its business in a quieter, less showy, way.

A tomato plants surface area is covered in hundreds of thousands of tiny hairs. These hairs trap insects, kill them and then allow the bodies to fall to the ground where the nutrients from the decaying corpse are slowly absorbed by the roots. It's believed that this started out as a defence mechanism to prevent insect infestations, but then developed through evolution into a survival mechanism for prospering in areas of poor soil.

So here we have something really interesting - two very different plants, killing and devouring the nutrients from insects to survive and prosper, but doing it in two very different ways.

I know what you're probably thinking though...very interesting, but if I want a botany lesson I'll watch David Attenborough. Bear with me, there is a devious purpose to all this.

You see, in business, everyone recognises and notices the Venus fly trap style marketing. It's the TV advertisements, the full page advertisements in newspapers and magazines, the grab-by-the-throat direct mail, the telesales pitch, the foot in the door salesman. And because of that, it's easy to believe that this is the only way to do things – the only way to prosper in a harsh and cut-throat environment.

But as the tomato plant amply demonstrates, there are other ways of going about things...ways that go largely unnoticed because they creep under the radar. But they're no less effective because of it.

Do you want an example? Well now, this may stretch your powers of visualisation to the limit, but I want you to imagine an online newsletter, written for free. Nobody is asked to pay to read it, and it's published quite regularly. The newsletter is designed to help people make more money, and people really seem to appreciate being able to read stuff like that. One chap (rather annoyingly) told the newsletter writer that he pulled in over £10 million with something he read in one of these newsletters. But as I say, it's all for free. No Venus fly trap style enticement, followed by a violent snap shut on the helpless credit card. Just a steady stream of useful information and insights, which you can access for free.

So what's the point?

Well I hope it won't disappoint you too much to learn that the motives of the person writing that newsletter might not be totally altruistic. At some point in the future, he may be hoping that he will be able to send you information on something that you'd quite like to buy. And the fact that you've been communicating regularly through his free newsletter makes it more likely that you will take the plunge, than would otherwise have been the case. It's a much slower process, but no less effective in its own way...

You get to know each other over a period of weeks and months, he provides you with plenty of free information and insights relating to something you're interested in, and as a result you build a bit more trust in me than you would if he was just a stranger coming out of the blue and trying to sell you something.

There's nothing manipulative or unethical about this though. It only works commercially if he provides you with useful, interesting and valid information for free. If he doesn't, you'll feel no more kindly towards him than if he was a complete stranger. So it's a classic win-win (or lose-lose) situation.

This is all purely hypothetical though....just the product of my fertile imagination!

Anyway, I don't want you to misunderstand what I'm saying here. I'm not suggesting you should scrap your 'fly trap' marketing in favour of the more low key 'tomato plant' approach - that you should abandon the quick kill in favour of the slow burn. But each has their place in an effective marketing strategy for any company or product. A Venus fly tap can only be a Venus fly trap, a tomato plant can only be a tomato plant. But as a marketer, you can be both.

Here's my suggestion – take an objective look at your marketing. Is it mainly fly trap or tomato plant in nature? Is it hard or soft...fast or slow...out in the open or under the radar? And whichever it is, are there ways you could employ to get the alternative approach working for you and making money? Is there a 'tomato plant' waiting to bear fruit in your business? Are there places where you can employ a 'down and dirty' fly trap to achieve a quick win?

Unless you have the perfect marketing machine driving your business forward, I'd be amazed if there isn't something you can put into practice here.

The Art Of Ethical Deception

Like most blokes of sound mind and a conventional sexual orientation, I rank shopping somewhere between having root canal treatment and learning cross stitch, in the order of things I most like to be doing on a Saturday morning. But also, like most blokes, I'm not always successful in avoiding it, which is why I found myself with my shopaholic daughter in the local shopping centre from hell a few weeks ago.

She was particularly keen to visit a store which has recently opened. It's called Hollister, and is part of the Abercrombie and Fitch group. Now I'd never heard of it before, let alone visited it, but was surprised to find that I'd actually walked past it quite a few times but hadn't realised. You see I'd assumed it was a restaurant or bar, because it looks nothing like any other mainstream shop you've ever seen.

The first thing you notice is the light - or rather the lack of it. From the outside the store looks like a surf shack with tiny windows and no evidence of any light from the inside. That's because there isn't any. To get into the store you enter through a narrow dark veranda-style hallway, which to the untrained eye looks like a waste of expensive retail space. You then enter through some double doors into what can best be described as gloom. There are no lights other than a few strategically placed spotlights, dimly lighting the merchandise just enough that you can get only a very vague idea of the shape and colour of what you're looking at.

I honestly couldn't tell whether I was looking at men's or women's clothes, and wouldn't have the night vision necessary to find my size. In short, it's the complete antithesis of everything I thought I knew about the most effective retail environment. Bright? Airy? Inviting? Spacious? Hollister is none of these…

And yet it's one of the world's most successful brands in its market sector. On the day I visited, the store was packed – and packed with just about the most homogeneous group of customers I think I've seen anywhere. The clientele was almost entirely middle class teens of both sexes. Even the staff were middle class teens. Not a chav in sight or an old person…apart from me standing in a corner feeling about as conspicuous as a Rastafarian at the BNP Christmas party. It's like they'd gone out into the street and physically rounded up the people they wanted and discarded the rest.

Now I stood there thinking that either...

1) This is all just a happy accident resulting in an outrageous success - an old established company adopted by a new group of consumers.

2) A very clever and calculated marketing machine with every detail carefully orchestrated and implemented.

I did a bit of research and found it's the latter. The impression conveyed is of an old established company. In fact the company even has a 'back story', which ties together all elements of the brand, revolving around one John M Hollister who established the company in 1922. He graduated from Yale University in 1915, before boarding a succession of steamboats and arriving in the Dutch West Indies in 1917. There he bought a rubber plantation and met his future wife, Meta. He later sold the plantation and bought a 50 ft Schooner, on which he and Meta spent two years sailing the south Pacific, before docking in Los Angeles in 1917 where they got married. John junior was born in 1922, and John senior started the Hollister store in Laguna Beach the same year selling furniture, jewellery and linen the Hollisters had fallen in love with on their South Pacific adventure. It was only in 1957, when John Jnr took over the company that the product line moved over to surf style apparel and equipment, which is a theme that runs through its inventory today.

Interesting story isn't it? But that's precisely what it is - a story created by the companies marketing department to help convey to both employees and customers, the ethos and values of the Hollister brand. There is no John Hollister (neither senior nor junior) and there never was. The less interesting truth is that the Hollister brand was created in the Abercrombie and Fitch marketing department some time in the late 1990's in the slightly less exotic Columbus, Ohio. The first store didn't open until 2000.

I think it's a demonstration of how far marketing has come, and how far it can go. Here's a company that not only made plans for the future, but also made plans for the past! They didn't have a heritage and so they created one, and then made sure that their present and future tied in with the heritage they'd created for themselves.

Is there a lesson for us as individuals and small-fry entrepreneurs here? I'm sure there is.

You see, you are what others perceive you to be. Objective reality may exist but it doesn't really matter. The objective reality of Hollister is that it was a brand thought up by some (probably) boring marketing bods in one of the least sexy parts of the United States a few years ago. The perception is that it was created by some adventurous, romantic young man almost a century ago, with links to some of the most exotic and evocative places on earth. It's the perception that matters, because that's what exists in the minds of the people that matter – the customers.

Your objective reality, and that of your business or enterprise, may be dull and boring, but the perception you create doesn't need to be. There's a thin line to be walked between self-serving deceit, and subtly creating a mutually beneficial impression, as Hollister have done, but it's one that's worth treading.

Hollister may not have been created in the first part of the 20th century, but if its products, ideals, ethos and approach are in harmony with the image it's created for itself, does that really matter? Is anyone harmed by being misled? The customers certainly don't seem to be complaining.

So is there some way you could subtly 'reinvent' your own history or that of the business or enterprise you run? Is there some way you can create an impression of the past, in line with the way you'd like to move forward into the future? And can you do it without over stepping the ethical line?

If you can, and you can then live up to your new image, then everyone can benefit. But if you overstep the mark, or create an impression which you then fail to live up to, you'll be labelled a fake and a charlatan. Miss-direction only ever benefits the perpetrator if all parties affected by it benefit too. Use it unethically or clumsily, and you'll simply end up worse off than if you'd never tried. The universe will see to that.

Not always easy this business lark, is it?

The New House Blues

I bought a house today. Nothing particularly unusual in that. Over the past 5 years or so I've bought about 70 properties and still have most of them. But this one has caused me more mental torment than most.

I should explain that I have a property business and all these properties - a mixture of houses, flats and commercial units - are let out to tenants. When I'm feeling stronger one day, I'll share some tales of the trials and tribulations of being a landlord. But my mental torment has nothing to do with that, because this property isn't let to tenants, and it's not going to be.

It's a property I've bought for personal use, and because of that, some of the decisions about the purchase weren't solely in my hands. You know how it is…someone (mentioning no names) falls in love with the place and must have it. This puts you in rather a different position from when you're taking a purely business decision on something. Then it's just a case of working out the numbers, making an offer and if it doesn't work out…next! But now emotions come into play - that and the realisation that if it the deal falls apart because of your 'penny pinching, (Can't believe I was accused of that!) You may find yourself eating beans out of a can for the next month.

Anyway, I was motivated to complete a deal on the house, but conscious of the need to pay the right price. My normal tactic of offering a price commensurate with the value of a 2 bed terrace in Darlington circa 1984 was not going to wash. And so I came up with an offer price which was challenging, but not insulting. What happened next is the source of my mental torment…

The offer was accepted!

Just like that. No haggling, no time taken to think about it, no if, buts or maybes. Just a quick acceptance of the offer. Arm duly snapped off.

Now what do you think my reaction was when that happened? What would your reaction be? If your brain is wired up like most of us, you'd probably think one of two things - and probably both in quick succession:

1. I offered too much. I could have got it cheaper.

2. Perhaps there's something wrong with it.

In the case of a property, the second thought can be dispensed with pretty easily via a survey and some due diligence on the area, neighbours and neighbourhood. But the first thought will stay with you for ever.

Negotiation is a massive subject, and not one I'm particularly skilled or knowledgeable in, but I do know this – if you accept the first offer you're made, you're doing neither party any favours. You won't get the maximum amount for what you're selling and the buyer will go away with the nagging feeling that he's over paid.

In any negotiation, you're looking to achieve a win-win situation – both buyer and seller getting what they want from the deal. By accepting the first offer, you're doing just the opposite. You're making the buyer feel uncomfortable, and potentially throwing money away at the same time. Paradoxically, my mental torment would have been reduced by being asked to pay a few thousand more! How counter-intuitive and illogical is that? And yet if you put yourself in the same position, I think you'd probably feel the same way.

Would I have actually paid any more? We'll never know, because nobody tried to find out. Maybe not. But at least everyone would feel more comfortable. The seller would know that the limit had been reached, and I'd know (or at least be made to think!) that my offer was right on the wire.

The next time you're negotiating the sale of anything, I'd urge you to keep this firmly in mind. You'll get a better deal for yourself and send the buyer away happier (if a little poorer) for the experience.

Doing It Write!

One of the things that seems to annoy people about me (of which there are many) is that I always insist on business propositions being presented in writing right from the start. The speculative phone calls come in on a daily basis.

"If I could just speak to him...it will only take a couple of minutes."

In the dim and distant past I would have taken phone calls like this, but now I know better. The typical response to my request to 'put it in writing' is usually something like...

"Well...erm...it's really hard to explain on paper."

Forcing someone to commit their idea or proposition to the written word, makes them think clearly about what they're offering. Experience tells me, that when someone says their idea is hard to commit to paper, it means one of two things. Either they haven't thought through and formulated the idea properly, or it will be too complex for customers to grasp easily. At some point I'm probably going to have to sell their idea through the written word, and if they can't even describe it in that medium, what chance will I have?

Committing words to paper (or pixel) fulfils another important brief too – it minimises the opportunity for misunderstanding. Perhaps, like me, you've had a conversation with someone and been astonished to find later that their interpretation and recollection of it, is completely different to yours. It's like you've had two separate conversations, but what's really happened is that you've each perceived the content of the conversation from the perspective of your individual experiences, interests and biases. If it's down on paper, the scope for misinterpretation is greatly reduced. There's one last very important reason for having things down in a form which can be read, and then re-read at a later date.

In his book, "59 Seconds – Think A Little, Change A Lot", author Richard Wiseman tells how he got a group of students at Carnell University to spend a week taking careful note of all their communications – face to face, on the phone, texts and emails. He then asked them to work through these communications, and identify how many contained lies.

The result, although not really surprising, is interesting and instructive. Wiseman found that people are far less likely to lie in emails than they are in more direct forms of unrecorded communication. The reason is obvious; the evidence of their words is tangible and can be referred to long after the conversation has taken place.

I don't have any empirical evidence to back this up (when did that ever stop me?) but have noticed a strong correlation between the type of people who are keen to have a telephone conversation about their 'wonder idea/proposition', and those who prove to have been economical with the truth when we get to the bottom of things. If you're going to lie, you won't want it in writing.

So written communication is almost always the best way to go...

1) It forces the parties to communicate in very clear terms about what is being offered/on offer.

2) It drastically reduces the chances of a misunderstanding.

3) It increases the chances of the content of the communication being true.

If you want your communications to be clear, conflict free and compliant with the facts (and why would you want anything else?) then there's only one effective solution...

Get it in writing!

Postscript

I hope you enjoyed the book, and at the very least it's given you some serious food for thought. I just want to finish by re-emphasising that there's nothing particularly special about the people who go out and make a great deal of money for themselves. They don't belong to some separate society or some secret club you've not been invited to join. Meet them, rub shoulders with them and you'll quickly discover that they're disappointingly ordinary.

So what IS their secret?

Well they do things differently to the crowd. Do the same as the crowd and you get what the crowd gets? Do different things to the crowd and you get something else? The exciting thing is that whilst not everyone can be unusual or special, (like a gifted academic, a talented singer, or a brilliant artist) anyone can learn how to do unusual things - to do something different from the crowd. And if you can do that, you can make a great deal of money for yourself. You'll find some information about another of my books after this postscript, which I think will help you in your quest for the unusual.

In closing, if you have any comments on what you've read here – good or bad –or suggestions for additional information you'd find useful, I'd be delighted to hear from you.

If you have an idea for a business project you'd like some feedback on, or a money making issue you'd like an opinion on, then don't hesitate to get in touch via the contact details below. I can't promise to have all the answers, but I might just be able to help.

Good luck and best wishes with whatever you do.

John Harrison

Streetwise Publications Ltd, Eden House, Genesis Park,
Sheffield Road, Rotherham S60 1DX
Tel: 01709 820033 Fax: 01709 360611
My email address is john@streetwisepublications.co.uk

Special Offer For Readers Of This Book Only

**The Highly Acclaimed Best Selling
Book By John Harrison...**

"The Toilet Pan Millionaire - Money Making Secrets You Can Learn On The Loo!"

"I Got Rich In The Last Economic Downturn, And Now I'm Going To Help You To Get Rich In This One!"

Dear Reader,

Get your head out from under the duvet, switch off the doom and gloom TV, and don't even <u>think</u> about battening down the hatches or heading for the hills.

Why?

Because if you do, you'll miss out on a huge opportunity – just like millions of 'sheep' blindly doing what everyone else is doing.

Here's what it's all about...

Watch TV or read the mainstream media, you'd be forgiven for thinking that economic Armageddon has descended upon all of us...that all resistance is futile.

Crap, crap and more crap! Here's the truth of it...

Some of the biggest financial fortunes in history have their roots in recession and economic downturn. Why? Because for every problem an economic downturn creates, an opportunity opens up. One man's distress sale is another mans bargain buy. People don't stop spending money...they just spend a little less in slightly different ways.

And with the sheep pathetically laying low and hoping it will all go away, there's little or no competition to get a foothold in the new order of things.

I started my business at the height of the last recession without a thought. Naïve? Maybe, but here's the thing I discovered...

You can still easily make life-changing money in a downturn. People don't stop spending. Yes, they spend a little less overall, and they cut back in certain areas. But...

They spend more on some stuff too!

And they're persuaded by different promotional appeals than when the good times are rolling. Adapt to that...and adaptation is the key...and a bonanza awaits.

With the scared sheep safely out of the way, it's open season for those of us who don't follow the heard (or should that be flock?) to steam in and start making money.

Want further proof?

Listen to the words of Warren Buffett - worth around $60 Billion, and one of the richest men in the world. Here's what he had to say about making money...

"Be fearful when others are greedy and greedy when others are fearful."

The time to be 'greedy'...to take advantage of what's happening is now. And that's why my latest book...

"The Toilet Pan Millionaire – Money Making Secrets You Can Learn Sitting On The Loo!"

has come at just the right time.

I know what you're probably thinking…"why the title?" Well let me get that out of the way first before I tell you what you can expect to learn in the book and reveal the obscenely low price I've reserved for you.

The book is an unashamed second volume of the highly acclaimed (if I say so myself) *'The Money Making Magic Of A Funfair Goldfish And Other Get Rich Secrets Of A Mattress-Bound Millionaire'*, and follows a similar format. That means short, easily digested chapters, many of which were originally designed and used as 'insider' training materials for a small group of people I've been individually mentoring to greater success.

How short? Well that's where the title of the book came from…

A business associate who read *The Money Making Magic Of A Funfair Goldfish* said he liked it because you could read a chapter and get an idea to act on while sat on the toilet. That wasn't exactly what he said, but I've edited his comments out of concern to the sensitivities of more gentile readers! Whilst I thought this said more about the state of his digestive system than the nature of the book, I knew what he meant.

And so *The Toilet Pan Millionaire – Money Making Secrets You can Learn Sitting on the Loo* was born.

It follows a similar pattern to its predecessor, and will maybe even appeal to those with a little more fibre in their diet – if you get my drift!

Over <u>300 pages</u>…<u>more than 90 chapters</u>…each containing an idea you can take away and use to enhance your wealth and success straight away. Here's what readers have said…

Reader Comments...

"Absolutely spot on and hilarious. I am now laughing, so you have made my day."
Linda Hayes

"Absolutely brilliant. A fantastic and truthful view of things as they are. This has really shaken me and hopefully I can get on and do something."
Ashley Burn

"Thanks for the sound advice. It made me realise that much to my shame, I have done exactly what you are describing in the past. I won't be making the same mistakes in the future."
Jenny Smith

*"Very funny. Absolutely spot on though.
Cheered me up no end."*
David White

"Great reading."
Roger Milne

"...made my day."
Marion Ryan

"Very enjoyable and humorous."
Marguerite Boyce

"Well done! Very Good! You're a brave man though. I think you may get a bit of hate mail. But that's life!"
Leslie Emms

"I will be instilling a spirit of entrepreneurship and critical reasoning in my boys as they grow up and will keep a copy of this for them to read and think about when they get older."
Richard Caswell

"You have articulated very nicely what I have been trying to put across to me children for the last few years. I think I will allow them to read this for themselves."
John McMyn

"Wonderful. I loved it"
Jill Luckham

*"It makes me smile and has some great ideas. Bound to make me better at my day job.
Should be required reading at school."*
Ian Muir

"A big thumbs up to you for this."
Peter Prescott

"Thanks for brightening up my Monday morning…a brilliant piece of writing."
Patricia Jones

"Love it!!! At last a man who thinks like I do."
Allyson Gale.

"You have made me and saved me a fortune over the last 15 or whatever it is years now."
John Newman

"Very, very good.! Fantastic really. It got me looking, and gave me some great ideas"
David Mesher

"…an elegant, modern parable from the book of John, which should become part of a new Business Bible."
Gordon Wilson

"Inspired. Thanks for a great series of information and inspiration. Whenever I read, there's always an aha! moment."
Dave Foster

"Excellent, very perceptive and very funny."
Bill Eaton

> *"Always thought provoking."*
> **Gary Stevens**

> *"I like your writing style. There are so many things to read, but your style is refreshing and holds the attention."*
> **John Winlow**

> *"I am about to embark on a new career from home with one of your recommendations."*
> **Ernie Simms**

> *"I read you for the first time today and I an all consumed."*
> **Bawa Attray**

> *"Funny and inspiring."*
> **Greg Jackson**

I've just remembered after reading these comments something I should have told you earlier. <u>This isn't some dry and boring business book</u>...full of sound information but dull as ditch water. As you'll see, people really seem to enjoy reading it – and I think that's important. I want you to learn something (and more importantly, act on what you've learned) but I want you to have a good time learning it too.

I guarantee that not only will you make money from what you read in *The Toilet Pan Millionaire,* but you'll have fun with it too. If you don't, then I insist that you ask for your money back. More about that later, but first I want to give you an idea of some of the things you're going to hear about in this unique book...

- How to <u>get rich in a recession</u>. I've done it before. Here's how to do it again! Many major fortunes have their roots in difficult times. Now's your chance.

- The secret of the worlds most successful author (bet you can't guess who it is!) and how you can use it to make a fortune in any business. I've <u>personally made millions</u> from this one idea.

- Why 'bad publicity' is often the very best kind…and how to create it without ruining your reputation.

- How listening to your customers could destroy your business…exploding the myth that 'the customer is always right.'

- What embarrassing bodies on TV taught me about overcoming the biggest single barrier to making a profit-yielding sale. Sometimes the best ideas come from the strangest places!

- The profit inducing secret I learned from my rowing machine and a Marks & Spencer sandwich. If you're not using this you're missing a massive opportunity.

- The truth about the 'worlds worst business' where 99% of prospects tell you to "*** off"…but makes millionaires from paupers!

- Why you need customers to hate you…and if they don't you're in trouble.

- How to legally imprison a customer, and refuse to let him leave with his wallet.

- What Einstein got wrong about making money and what Newton got right. The astonishing story of what the laws of Physics teach us about getting rich. (If you don't know this, you're guaranteed to fail every time.)

- The truth about luck I learned from Paul Daniels…and how to attract all the luck you'll ever need.

- The great pie secret. Every entrepreneur needs to know about pies, but most don't have a clue.

- The money making lesson hidden in a children's egg and spoon race. (If you see others doing better and don't know why – the answer is probably here)

- What a <u>pro wrestler taught me</u> about marketing to real people. This will force you to see new and exciting opportunities in any bog standard product.

- The <u>highly controversial</u> truth about a 'magic policeman' who may be wrecking your chances of success...and what you need to do to cast him aside. (Skip this chapter is easily offended!)

- Why you must learn how to market to <u>vain, greedy sex-obsessed monsters</u>. (The reason will almost certainly shock and offend you!)

- The great audience question (Learn whether you're in the right business...or need to start again...in an instant)

- The secret ingredient that almost <u>forces and compels</u> your customers to find out more about you and your products. Anyone can use this but it's rarely, if ever, talked about. It beats talking about 'benefits' by a mile.

- Why Paul McCartney, Burt Bacharach and David Bowie should make you rejoice (and excited) that you haven't got started in your new business yet. What they have in common isn't a secret, but nobody seems to have noticed it!

- Why <u>saving money is for morons</u>...and there are an awful lot of them about!

- The destructive <u>subliminal message</u> in film, TV and media which you must be consciously aware of if it's not to cruelly sabotage your efforts to get rich.

- How to determine <u>your real age</u>. The answer will almost certainly stun you, and give you a new lease on life.

- The hidden danger in a good education...and what to do to protect yourself from harm.

- How being hard to please could make you rich. <u>The Simon Cowell secret</u>, and how you can use it to transform your fortunes.

- How to boost your profits by turning away customers. It's counter-intuitive, but it works!

- The <u>one question</u> people want answering above all others. It won't come as a shock, but what it means for you almost certainly will.

- What <u>Jack Lemmon</u> said about elevators. There are million pound fortunes ready to spring from his words, and yours could be one of them.

- The <u>three simple questions</u> you need to ask yourself about any new venture. It will take less than a minute and the answers will reveal instantaneously whether you should proceed.

- The money making secret <u>revealed by Karl Marx</u> (of all people!) and how you can use it to turn a struggling business into a fortune maker. Apply this to any business and watch the cash pour in.

- How to speak to your customers in language they'll understand - and have them reaching for their wallets. Most businesses do just the opposite.

- The <u>Duke of Wellington test</u>…How to tell if you're cut out to be a successful entrepreneur.

- Why lottery winners are miserable…but why I still want to win. And you should too!

- The lesson of Gordon and Alf…pay close attention to this and it will have a monumental effect on the impact your words have on prospective customers. (Clue: Sometimes less is more.)

- What have the Okinawa Islanders and a Formula One car got in common? The answer reveals something incredibly powerful about wealth and success.

- The <u>common thread</u> that links Margaret Thatcher and Dennis Skinner…and why you need to be more like Tony Blair or

David Cameron if you want to amass more cash than you can count.

- The secret I learned from a hearing aid salesman that you'd be crazy to ignore. <u>Add 50% to your profits</u> in weeks by using this.

- How to become a 'method marketer'. It works for actors and it can work for you too. I had to get very uncomfortable to learn use this, and you might too.

- How to uncover, rediscover and exploit your hidden skills and abilities. Don't think you've got any? <u>Prepare for a shock</u>.

- The off-the-wall relationship between effort and reward which all successful entrepreneurs know, but are alien to 99% of employees. (It's nothing to do with hard work!)

- Why getting a degree can be <u>worse than useless</u>...and how to 'recover' if you already have one.

- The character flaw shared by Al Capone and Heather Mills...and what it tells us about the one thing <u>you must never say to a customer</u> if you want them to buy from you.

- What Moby and me (but not together!) did to get rich. If you're struggling to stand out you need to read about this now.

- Why 'intelligent' people wind up broke, and <u>thickies' often prosper</u>.

- What Marie Antoinette knew about business that most entrepreneurs don't. Ignore this and you face a world of pain and disappointment. Take it on board and it's like someone just gave you an <u>immediate upgrade to the fast track.</u>

- Why you need to be greedy...but only at the right time. And it's not when you think. Switch on your greed gland at the right moment and a fortune awaits.

- How to <u>demolish</u> the physical and psychological barriers that stop cash flooding from your customer's bank account to yours. This works for any business dealing with the public.

- The counter-intuitive and shocking truth about giving customers choice. How to boost your profits by making your customers decisions for them.

- What I learned about success from a <u>famous actor</u> while I was letting him out of jail. (Really!) You're going to have a massive 'aha' moment when you read about this.

And with chapters like…

- Man Sets Fire To Friends Head (Chapter 11)
- My Manchester United Debut (Chapter 44)
- Duncan Bannatyne's Paper Round (Chapter 45)
- Where Heather Mills Meets Al Capone (Chapter 49)
- CU 2Moz…You Idiot (Chapter 27)
- Brian Blessed's Blinkers (Chapter 53)
- The Yorkshire Pudding Myth (Chapter 55)
- Rich Folk Are Plonkers Too. (Chapter 58)
- The Cow Heal And Tripe Road To Ruin (Chapter 68)
- Roger Mellie Lives (Chapter 83)
- A Little Known Use For A Dwarf (Chapter 85)
- Harrison & The Saga Louts

…You're unlikely to get bored!

<u>Order your copy of *"The Toilet Pan Millionaire – Money Making Secrets You Can Learn On The Loo"*…Today!</u>

To receive your copy of the book
you can call one of our credit card hotlines
on: 01709 361819 (phone) or 01709 360611 (fax) or visit
<u>www.streetwisenews.com/tpm</u>

And it comes at a truly bargain price. I've set the price really low because I want to get this out to as many people as I can, as quickly as possible. So as an existing reader you can get hold of a copy for just £29.95...

But it gets better...

Because I've arranged for you to receive a £10 discount, leaving just £19.95 to pay!

And better...

You see, I only want you to pay for this if you enjoy it and find it useful. That's why I'm including a...

Cast Iron 30 Day Money Back Guarantee

You can order 'The Toilet Pan Millionaire in complete confidence. If you're unhappy with it for any reason whatsoever, or can't see how you can put the insider information it contains to use, then you can simply return it within 30 days and receive a prompt and courteous refund of every penny you've paid. Is that fair?

I desperately want to get this information out to as many people who need it as possible. That's why I'm making this guarantee totally unequivocal and completely 'catch-free'. I don't want there to be a single reason why you don't get to look at this. It's totally unconditional. You can return the book for any reason, or no reason at all.

So when you order a copy of the book on approval, it's without any risk or obligation. If you decide it's not for you, then you get to read it for free. A risk for me as the author? Maybe. But it's a risk worth taking to get this into your hands, and don't think you'll even think about returning it once you get hold of a copy.

I look forward to despatching your copy of my new book and hearing what you think about it.

Kind Regards

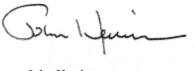

John Harrison

PS. Don't forget, if you order your approval copy <u>within 24 hours</u>, you'll get a £10 discount on the usual purchase price, leaving just £19.95 to pay.

PPPS Just one more thing. If you're one of the <u>first 100 people</u> to order a copy, I'll sign it for you. Not sure if that might be a deterrent rather than an incentive, but it's there all the same.

How To order Your Copy On Approval:

Visit <u>www.streetwisenews.com/tpm</u>

or you can call one of our credit card hotlines on
01709 361819 (phone) or 01709 360611 (fax).

The Streetwise Bulletin

Your Free Daily Email Newsletter

Despite what the gloom-mongers might tell you, there are more money making, investment and wealth building opportunities around now than ever before. You wouldn't believe the amount of top notch information that floods into our office every day, and much of it lays unused and unloved

Often we receive a piece of information that needs acting upon right away. At other times we get an insider tip on something which might make you a few hundred quid, but isn't worth creating a full blown product around. And then there's other stuff which would normally slip through the net because, well, we're just so busy.

That was the background for the launch of The Streetwise Bulletin in 2010, a free daily email newsletter published each week day.

There's nothing to buy here. Just interesting, empowering and useful information you can use straight away. I share the writing and revealing with Ian Maitland, who has over 20 years experience in the home business, investment, property and marketing fields. Ian really has his ear to the ground on everything 'money' and brings in red hot information every day. I pitch in as well – plus attempt to lighten the load a little with the sort of insights and questionable humour you'll find in my books and Blogs. You've been warned!

Here's an example of a few articles from the past few weeks:

Dating With A Difference

If you're looking for a solid and enduring business, you can't do much better than get involved with something which caters for a basic human need. It's for that reason that eFlirt Expert seems to be on solid ground from the start.

Dating has always been a pitfall-strewn activity, and the move over the past few years, to a situation where a lot of the early moves take place on line, has only added to the difficulties. eFlirt Expert was set up to help people create the most favourable online persona through a combination of profile creation, photograph selection and email writing. The service doesn't stop there though, as it helps the individual manage the transition to real world dating. Apart from the regular dating and wardrobe advice, there's even a shadowing service, where a member of the team discretely follows the customer on a date and gives feedback and support.

Needless to say, this is an American service only available in New York and Boston at the moment. Might there be a market for something similar here in the UK?

Subscription Success

Here's the secret to a large number of small businesses...find something that people like, and then get them to commit to buying it regularly through a subscription, and you're guaranteed to make profit in the long run.

We all know how this model works in the publishing world for example, but it's much more widespread and versatile than that. For example, one company we recently came across (Bonbon) market a range of lip balms. For £5 a month, customers sign up to receive a different flavour every 12 times a year. If you're not into the product, this may seem a 'balmy' idea (no booing at the back please!) but with each customer worth £60 a year, you don't need too many to create a viable business.

There must be hundreds of products which would lend themselves to this kind of subscription service treatment. Anything edible, consumable or collectable has potential. Is there something you currently sell that could be given the subscription treatment? Do you currently buy something that would lend itself to this? I'm going to give some serious though to this myself, so you'd better get moving if you want to beat me to the best ideas!

Life Capture Profits

Do you know what people are interested in more than anything else? Themselves! This simple fact goes a long way to explain the popularity of what might be called 'life capture' products. They're products that enable the individual to record or document some aspect of their life, whether that be via the written word, audio, video or something else.

The latest product we've spotted (yours for about £130 on Amazon) is the Looxcie - a Bluetooth style video camera, which fits over the ear and points where the wearer is looking and therefore records everything he or she sees. If something interesting happens, they simply press a button to save it, so that it can be later uploaded to Mac or PC – and even emailed to a pre- set list of contacts. Otherwise, the Looxcie records in a continuous loop, purging the earlier footage.

I mention this for three reasons:

1. *There seems no end to the life capture phenomenon at the moment. Is there some aspect of your product or offering that would enable you to cash in on it?*
2. *If the device took off, just imagine the amount of footage that would become available, and the potential creative opportunities that would bring. Could you make the first Looxcie film?*

3. *You might just want one, and if you do (and have a lot of female friends with a penchant for low cut tops or short skirts) I'll be happy to check out the quality of your footage for free.*

The Non-Meat Butcher

You don't have to be an out and out vegetarian to be interested in meat substitutes. Many meat eaters are also looking for ways in which they can eat more healthily (while still getting their 'fix') and it's for that reason that a vegetarian butcher starts to make sense.

The first vegetarian butcher, specialising in a wide range of meat substitutes like Soya, Tofu and Lupin (yes Lupin!) opened it's doors in The Hague, Holland recently. The target market is both vegetarians, and upmarket consumers who have decided for health reasons to substitute at least some of their meat eating for an alternative —and are prepared to pay a premium price to do it.

Could this take off in the UK? I'm just not sure at the moment, but it's a situation worth keeping an eye on. It wouldn't surprise me at all to see a small chain of vegetarian butchers operating in upmarket areas of the UK within the next few years. It would delight me if it was one of our readers who made it happen.

The Lessons Of Page 99

It's not so long ago that, if you'd written a book and wanted an opinion on it, the best you could do was hand it to a few friends or family members to see what they thought. Better than nothing, but it's hardly an unbiased and representative sample of the market, now is it?

It's with this problem in mind that a web based service called Page 99 was launched. The name of the service comes from the fact (which incidentally, is new to me) that when readers are scanning a book to decide whether to buy, they often flick to page 99 and base their decision on what they find there.

The site enables authors to upload page 99 of their book. Readers are then invited to go there and offer an unbiased opinion of whether what they've just read would persuade them to turn the page or buy the book. At a later stage, it's anticipated that the service will be expanded to incorporate full chapters, and I'd imagine that the site owners will then attempt to monetise the site by charging a fee for obtaining publishing deals, or maybe even offering the books directly as downloads themselves.

There seem to be a few ideas to take from this:

1. *If you have a book you'd like to get published, this could provide invaluable market research for you.*

2. *If you're an aspiring or established publisher, it could be a source of new material*

3. *There may be lucrative spin off opportunities in adjacent markets. What other 'product' could you enable people to sample free online, giving the producer valuable feedback, whilst creating an opportunity to make money for yourself?*

Calculated Profits

It's not unusual for groups of consumers to have quite transient needs, and when this happens, a business opportunity often opens up. Students are one such group. They often study a subject for a short period, and are required to source quite expensive resources, which they will only need for a short period of time. Previously, we've talked about services set up to rent books to students, thereby negating the need for them to make an expensive purchase.

A Canadian company has spotted another need they can satisfy in a similar way – by renting out expensive graphic and financial calculators. Students often need these for just a couple of classes and can save 70% by renting rather than buying. When the rental period is complete, they simply mail them back to the company.

I don't think this is a fortune-maker, but it could certainly be a solid business. As far as I know, nobody is doing this in the UK yet, so perhaps something to copy?

If you like the look of the sort of information you get in The Streetwise Bulletin, and would like to receive it in your inbox each day, simply go to:

www.streetwisenews.com/signup

and leave your email address. We'll do the rest.

For legal reasons we are obliged to state the following:

Disclaimer: to the fullest extent permitted by law, the sellers are providing this written material, its subsidiary elements and its contents on an 'as is' basis and make no (and expressly disclaim all) representations or warranties of any kind with respect to this material or its contents including, without limitation, advice and recommendations, warranties or merchantability and fitness for a particular purpose. The information is given for entertainment purposes only. In addition, we do not represent or warrant that the information accessible via this material is accurate, complete or current. To the fullest extent permitted by law, neither of the sellers or any of its affiliates, partners, directors, employees or other limitation compensatory, direct, indirect or consequential damages, loss of data, income or profit, loss of or damage to property and claims of third parties.